Families

BLACK AND CATHOLIC · CATHOLIC AND BLACK

READINGS, RESOURCES, AND FAMILY ACTIVITIES

SR. THEA BOWMAN, FSPA, PH.D., EDITOR

Commission on Marriage and Family Life
Department of Education
United States Catholic Conference

In its 1985 planning document, as approved by the general membership of the United States Catholic Conference in November 1984, the Department of Education and its Desk for Family Life Ministry were authorized to conduct a listening process directed toward black Catholic families, in order to produce a practical resource tool that would support them, as members of the Catholic Church. After much consultation, this current resource, *Families: Black and Catholic, Catholic and Black*, has been developed to help all Catholics foster an appreciation of the strengths and challenges of black Catholic families. The text has been reviewed and approved by Rev. Thomas G. Gallagher, Secretary of Education, in consultation with Rev. Thomas Lynch, Representative for Family Life Ministry, and is authorized for publication by the undersigned.

Monsignor Daniel F. Hoye
General Secretary
NCCB/USCC

June 6, 1985

EDITOR'S NOTE

Due to the anthological nature of this publication, it was necessary to retain the original capitalization of many of the words found herein. Therefore, let the reader be advised that the word *Black/black* appears in both the capitalized and lower-case forms throughout this anthology. In no way does the capitalization (or lack thereof) add to or detract from the word and its usage.

Acknowledgments

I would like to thank the Office of Publishing and Promotion Services of the United States Catholic Conference (USCC); all of the contributors, encouragers, and supporters; Suzanne Elsesser, executive editor; Charles Buggé of the USCC Office of Copyrights and Permissions; Sr. Angela Williams, OSF, artist; and the network of Black Catholic family. I am also grateful to the following persons and organizations that donated photos: The Campaign for Human Development (CHD), USCC; Rogelio Solis and *Mississippi Today,* Diocese of Jackson; the John Reese Family, Jackson, Miss.; *Southern Cross,* Diocese of San Diego; Joyce Smith, Cincinnati, Ohio; and Marian College, Indianapolis, Ind. I especially thank Bishop James P. Lyke, OFM, Ph.D., without whose efforts this project would have died of inertia.

To the Bowmans and to all my mothers, fathers, grandparents, uncles, aunts, sisters, brothers, cousins, nieces, nephews, children, in-laws, outlaws; to all who have loved and nurtured me; to all with whom I am related by blood and/or commitment; and especially to Fr. Joseph Roy Nearon, SSS—my father, teacher, brother, friend.

Sr. Thea

Table of Contents

CHD/Peter Magubane

CHD/Peter Magubane

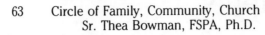

PART III: OUR RESPONSE

PART IV: WE SHARE

CHD/Barbara Baker Stephenson

Foreword

From my pastoral experience, I have learned that whatever the Church does to preach the Gospel and carry on its ministry ultimately relies upon the family for effectiveness and duration. If the families in a parish are spiritually strong, then the soil for the Word of God will be a rich grounding for the mustard seed of the Kingdom.

Sister Thea Bowman's *Families: Black and Catholic, Catholic and Black* is a welcome and significant contribution to the life of the Church in the Black community precisely because it is an affirmation of family life, as well as an instrument to develop and sustain this life. This support is particularly needed at this time because the state of family life within our nation and within the Black community is experiencing serious difficulties. As the Black Bishops of the United States note in the pastoral letter, *What We Have Seen and Heard*:

> The heart of the human community is the family. In our society today, traditional family values are openly questioned and rejected. For many reasons, the Black family has been especially assailed, despite the importance that families still have in the Black cultural and spiritual tradition.

Black families and the pastoral staffs who serve them will find in Sister Thea's book a fine resource and stimulating text for family discussion and parish catechesis.

Bishop James P. Lyke, OFM, Ph.D.
Auxiliary Bishop of Cleveland

CHD/Michal Heron

Introduction

Sr. THEA BOWMAN, FSPA, Ph.D.

This book is by Black people from Black families for Black people from Black families.

It assumes that the Black family is alive and well. It assumes further that we as a people need to find ways old and new to walk and talk together; to bond more surely; to extend family more widely and effectively, so that no one is fatherless, motherless, sisterless, or brotherless; so that no one lacks the life-sustaining human support of family.

It attempts to help us maintain and strengthen Black rootedness, Black traditions and rituals whereby faith and values are transmitted and celebrated in family, in extended family, in intimate person-to-person exchange—mother to son, grandchild to grandpa, play brother to younger sister, friend to friend, member to member, and family to family. And whereby faith and values are transmitted and celebrated in casual conversation, in reminiscence and testimony, in song and dance, and in ritual and story.

It encourages Black families to think and talk about ourselves; our faith; our lived experience of family, Blackness, and Catholicism. It encourages us to think and talk about our dreams, goals, and aspirations; our concrete plans for being family and community, and for sharing our gift of Blackness with the Church.

It attempts to provide suggestions and resources for oral/aural family and community centered interactions, for talking, laughing, praying, and playing as we learn together.

This book is also for people of any color or culture who have chosen to be family with us, to join with us and walk with us and minister with us. We hope that it will help them to get to know us better.

It is designed for people who come into our communities to be Church with us, but who do not understand, sometimes do not realize they do not understand, and sometimes do not seem to want to understand what we think, feel, believe, and love about family, community, and Church. And it is for people who dwell on the "decline" or "disintegration" of Black family without seeing or intuiting its strength and breadth and beauty.

I hope this book will help these people to walk and talk and work with Black families and to listen sensitively and persistently so that they can engage in a true mutuality of ministry and evangelization; so we can change and grow and be community and Church together. I hope it will help them to raise the questions, to know the resources, and to engage in conversation with us, so that they learn about us. For it is only by walking and talking with us, learning and living with us, that they can be enabled to minister with and to us.

Too often, white people come to us with the answers to our problems. They don't bother to try to find out who we are, how we think, and what we're about. Too often, people who come to help do not realize that Black family is alive and well and that even when broken, even when hurting, it fosters deep faith and forges strong bonds.

Courtesy of the John Reese Family

This book brings together under one cover:

- the thoughts and concerns of Black folks of various faiths and perspectives who have thought deeply about the plight and potential of Black family;
- the reflections of Black Catholics on Black family and faith, Black family and Catholicism, the Church and the salvation of the family, Black families and the salvation of the Church;
- factual data;
- information about a cross section of resources—human, print, and media;
- people to begin to know;
- articles to read, but, more important, to think and talk about;
- songs to sing and poems to meditate on;
- things to make and do together;

- activities useful to family and Church;
- pictures, charts, and graphics to jog memory and consciousness and to stimulate dialogue;
- ideas to remind families to make time and take time together—quality time—and to be present and alive to one another through bonding and knowing, loving and growing, as family.

This book suggests a methodology of inquiry, a modality of sharing, and instruction based on the traditional oral/aural person-centered pedagogy of Black America. I hope that church groups and families will read it together, will contemplate and understand, adapt and use it together.

I hope it will help you think
pray
play
dream
plan
yearn
act
live
learn
and celebrate
together as family.

God be with you.

PART I

Here We Are

Here We Are!
Let the Church say
Amen.
Let the Church say
Hallelujah.
Let the Church say
Thank you, Jesus.
Amen.

Listen to the Blood

LERONE BENNETT, JR., PH.D.

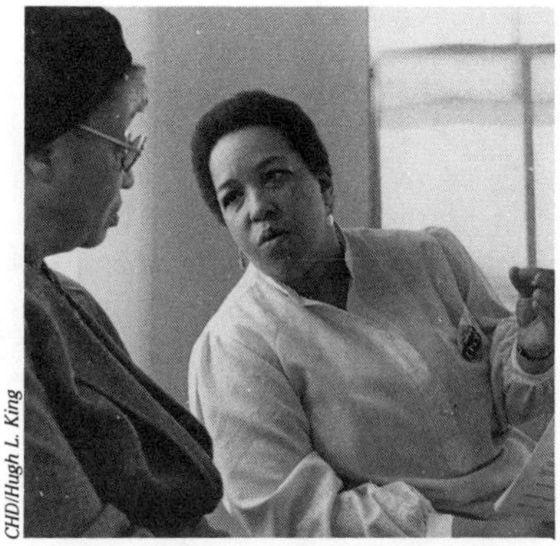
CHD/Hugh L. King

African-Americans didn't come to America. Who came to America? Millions of Africans from different national and linguistic groups. And although they came as individuals, they came from the same historical space and shared certain broad cultural and philosophical presuppositions. And when these individuals stepped off the ship, they stepped into a new historical space with three or four historical imperatives that were addressed to them personally. The first imperative was survival. And the second, growing out of the first, was the creation of a people, a social group or, if you please, a nation. And the record shows that our African fathers and mothers met that challenge. In the unpromising setting of the Slave Rows of America, and in the free Black communities of Philadelphia and Boston and New York, our founding fathers and mothers remade themselves as they remade America, creating a new synthesis, in part African, in part European, in part X. And the creation of that synthesis, and the creation of the foundations of America, were two of the greatest flights in the history of the human spirit. If our ancestors had done nothing else, they would have a claim on us and on history. But, astonishingly, they did do something else. For there was another challenge in their situation, the challenge of freedom. That challenge, that meaning, was not imposed on the situation; it was the meaning of the situation. And in order to give meaning to that meaning, African-Americans were forced by their circumstances to struggle for a deepening of the meaning of freedom in America. We know what that struggle has meant, and what it is, and if we want to get a historical perspective on our situation, we need only imagine what historians would say if the slaves (the external proletariat, to appropriate Toynbee's phrase) of Rome had changed the Roman Empire as much as African-Americans have changed the most powerful empire in the history of the world. That struggle is by no means over. The struggles of slavery and the Civil War and the Reconstruction and the sixties were stages on the road to an unfulfilled meaning that lies before us like our own shadows projected on a wall.

And what gives our history its grandeur and makes it of moment to the peoples of the world is the strategically important but hard and unpromising ground on which it is unfolding. It would be an exaggeration, but not much of an exaggeration, to say that never before has history given a people such a staggering task. Never before has a minority, and a racial minority at that, faced the historical necessity of transforming a country as technologically advanced as the United States of America. The burden is without parallel; so is the responsibility; so is the danger. And here, as elsewhere, the danger is a guarantee of the greatness. This may not be, as DuBois said, the last great battle of the West, but it is certainly one of the great and ennobling struggles of the West.

PASSING THE BATON

And so, at long last, we are in a position to look Dubois's question in the face. He asked— Remember? —what shall our suffering and triumphs and trials mean. And my answer to that question is that the meaning of our history, like the meaning of all history, is in process, and that it is up to us to create the meaning that we already are, by deepening the furrows of a meaning that has been given to us. There is nothing deep or mystical about this. We have all seen relay races on TV in which several men run one race by covering a certain amount of territory and then pass the baton on to another runner who repeats the same process. This same dynamic is at work on a deeper and more desperate level in the rhythm of the generations. For peoples, races, and nations advance on the shoulders of succeeding generations. One generation runs as fast as it can and then passes the baton on to another generation which runs as fast as it can and then passes the baton on, ad infinitum.

And it is easy to see from all this that each generation is dependent not only on the generations immediately preceding and following but on all the

Lerone Bennett, Jr., Ph.D., senior editor of *EBONY,* has lectured throughout the United States and was a delegate to the Sixth Pan-African Congress and the Second World Festival of Black and African Art. His poems, short stories, and articles have appeared in many periodicals and books and have been translated into French, German, Japanese, Swedish, Russian, and Arabic.

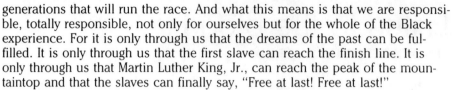

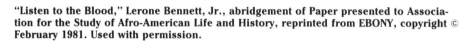

generations that will run the race. And what this means is that we are responsible, totally responsible, not only for ourselves but for the whole of the Black experience. For it is only through us that the dreams of the past can be fulfilled. It is only through us that the first slave can reach the finish line. It is only through us that Martin Luther King, Jr., can reach the peak of the mountaintop and that the slaves can finally say, "Free at last! Free at last!"

What does it all mean?

It is up to us to decide what it means by what we say, by what we write, by what we do. It is up to you, it is up to me, it is up to us, working together, to make sure that the slaves and the sharecroppers and the martyrs and victims did not bleed and dream and die in vain.

There is no meaning for the Black living or the Black dead or the Black unborn outside the great Black chain of that hope.

"Listen to the Blood," Lerone Bennett, Jr., abridgement of Paper presented to Association for the Study of Afro-American Life and History, reprinted from EBONY, copyright © February 1981. Used with permission.

Self-Identity A Christian Concept

BISHOP MOSES B. ANDERSON, SSE, D.D.

Living and surviving in the crucible of the slavery experience, Blacks did not live a marginal existence of survival. We took the cultural values which we brought to a foreign land and produced a self-concept which is called *soul* or *negritude*.

This soul or negritude is the essence of the Black experience. It is the connective skein that runs throughout the totality of the Black experience, weaving it together, making it intelligible, and giving it meaning. The task of the Black community has been to take its own culture and the consciousness of its own culture in order to define its own self. The remains of an antecedent culture that regards the whole world as a sacred cosmos is basic to the Black Self-Concept.

The Self-Concept of Blacks is not opposed to the Universality of the Church. In truth, it is the affirmation of authentic diversity which ensures Catholicity or Universality in the Church.

What we have witnessed in our time has been a reappropriation of all that is wholesome for Blacks. The slogans Black Power and Black Is Beautiful made vocal demonstrative gestures for what Blacks had been saying about themselves in their songs, dances, art, politics and plays, all of which take on the nature of a religious drama. The slogans did not create something de novo, something entirely new, they only summed up what was unspoken in the hearts of Black people. They said **I AM** in bold capital letters, not out of hatred, but with a sense of what God had done to set us free, to be a people, to be free, to be a person, to be self. Along with this gesture went the ardent plea for Blacks to cease to be "spooks," to be invisible—rather, to be one's self, to be one's own self.

There was the call to study one's own culture, to experience anew those events in our history before God, in order to recapture on an explicit level all that was and is our own. Blacks called upon Blacks to "wholeify" their lives, and to "holify" their being as a people. Black theologians as well as socioeconomic and political leaders urged all to give full expression to the Black Is Beautiful doctrine which was codified in the concept of soul or negritude.

When Blacks say soul, it brings to our minds the whole history of Black folks as it was actively experienced and fused together. It reminds us of what was brought from the mother country, Africa, and what has occurred within North America. It is experienced as a reality connected and interwoven and pregnant with a cosmic view of self in a foreign land. Soul reaffirms self when no one else cares, but Jesus. Soul allows one to discover, and to uncover, one's own ground of being, to shout, to strut, free. It says, sit when you want to sit, sit where you want to sit, and "Don't you let nobody turn you 'round." Soul is the language of Black folk, spoken and unspoken. It is the predisposition in Black folk that equips us to participate actively in all that the Gospel presents, in a truly human way. It allows us to approach the Gospel as subject to subject, not as subject to object. There is an active and vital participation in the Faith and the indigenization of the Self-Concept. The Self-Concept must keep in mind the prior wholesome conditions of those to whom the message of Christ is directed. If the Self of Christ is the word to be accepted in the biblical sense and in the Afro-American sense, it must be spoken in such a way that Afro-Americans may hear him in their own "Tongue." The Self-Concept must take our psychophysical "ground" into consideration.

Thus, Self-Concept of the mystical Christ presupposes indigenization. It must affirm the total body-soul relationship of a particular people. The wedding of the word to the hearer must take place. It is not, and has never been, enough that one will be able to memorize slogans. What is learned must be-

CHD/Peter Magubane

Bishop Moses B. Anderson, SSE, D.D., a member of the Society of St. Edmund, is an auxiliary bishop of the Archdiocese of Detroit. He has been vice-president of St. Michael College, Winooski, Vermont, and director of religious affairs at Xavier University in New Orleans. His writing includes papers and lectures on Black theology, indigenization of evangelization, racism, Black awareness, and Black spirituality.

come one with the hearer. This cannot take place unless there is a congruency between what is heard and the hearer. But to hear supposes a disposition to hear, and words which at least are analogous to one's own. This sort of Self-Concept is founded on the principle that a thing is perceived according to the mode of the receptor. This philosophical principle is in perfect agreement with our doctrine of grace. Grace completes what is, already, and gives it a share in the transcendent. God prepares us according to our nature in order to assist and elevate that nature to a transcendent position. In the notion of transcendency, there is not a creation *ex nihilo*, or the leaving aside of what is already there, but a completion of the nature which lacked something integral to its wholeness—one's participation in God's fullness.

"Self-Identity: A Christian Concept," Moses B. Anderson, SSE, from *Theology: A Portrait in Black*, Thaddeus J. Posey, OFM Cap., editor, copyright © 1980 National Black Catholic Clergy Caucus, Washington, D.C. Reprinted with permission.

Black families are among the strongest and most resilient institutions in the nation. Were it not so, we would not have survived as a people, and the national society would be even more inhuman and inhumane than it is.

Andrew Billingsley, Ph.D.
Black Families and the Struggle for Survival

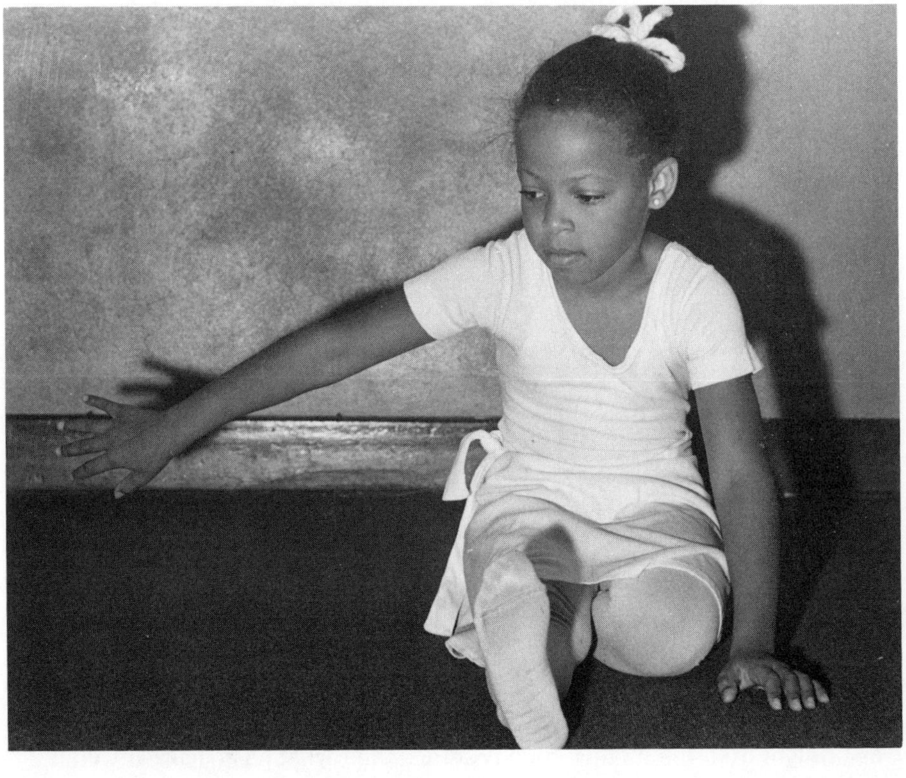

Rogelio Solis/Courtesy of Mississippi Today

Black American Families
with roots in Africa, Asia, Europe
North America, South
America, the Islands,
all of the above.
Black American Families
carrying proudly
reverently
meekly
sadly silently
defiantly
collectively
the heritage of ancient Africa
the Middle Passage
Slavery
Reconstruction
Migration
Segregation
the Movement for
Liberty
Life
Love

BLACK CATHOLICS

Christians
baptized in Christ Jesus
and guided by His Spirit
united in faith and worship
sharing Sacraments, living signs
of His living presence in our
world
building up His Body
continuing His Sacred Mission
as prophet—proclaiming God's
Word
priest—celebrating, worshiping
servant—ministering to the peoples
of the world
Witnessing (together with
The Holy Father
Bishops
Priests and Deacons
Lay Men and Women and Children
Everywhere)
that God is Love

large families small families nuclear families
extended families single-parent families adopted families
foster families augmented families makeshift families
Southern Northern Eastern Western families
rural or urban families suburban families
inner city, central city, ghetto families
Fifth Avenue or mansion families condominium families
apartment families project families
shotgun-house families duplex families laboring families
farming families business families professional families
academic families artistic families athletic families
fishing, swimming and relaxing families
uptight families together families
happy healthy families whole families
patriarchal families matriarchal families
anarchical families syncretic families
rich families poor families working families jobless families
middle-class,
upper middle-class,
upper-upper middle-class families
old established families aristocratic families
nouveau riche families moving-on-up families
educated, urbane, cultured families
opera-going families poetry-reading families
finger-snapping, gospel-loving, shouting, testifying families
shucking and jiving families fussing and fighting families
oppressed families disadvantaged families
struggling families disenfranchised families
disheartened families hurting families
separated families broken families mobile families
stay-at-home, stick-in-the-mud families
jet-setting, pace-setting, go-getting,
keeping-up-with-the-Joneses families
high society families
ebony families sable, swarthy families
brown, chocolate, caramel and/or tan families
mahogany and cinnamon, nutmeg and brown sugar,
bronze, red, tan, magnolia or honeydew
coal black or passé blanche
mixed families mixed-up families
multicolored, multitonal
curly headed, straight haired, Afroed families

When We Think of Family . . .

ANDREW BILLINGSLEY, Ph.D.

We know that when we think of family in the Black community, we do not confine our thinking—for our experience is not confined—to husband and wife and two children living together in splendid isolation in their own house. We are a more complex and humane people than that. And so the extended family and a multiple variety of nuclear, extended, and augmented family forms are an intricate part of what we mean by family. And it must be clear to all of us, as a basis for all we attempt to say and do in the interest of human development, that were it not for the strength, endurance, adaptability, and resilience of family life in the Black community, we would not have survived as a people.

Black Families and the Struggle for Survival, Andrew Billingsley, copyright © 1974 Friendship Press, New York, N.Y. Used by permission.

Andrew Billingsley, Ph.D., is professor of sociology and Afro-American studies at the University of Maryland. A former president of Morgan State University in Baltimore, he was visiting scholar and professor of social welfare at the Institute for the Study of Social Change of the University of California, Berkeley. His extensive writing includes the influential *Black Families in White America* (Prentice-Hall), *Children of the Storm* (Harcourt, Brace) and *Black Families and the Struggle for Survival* (Friendship Press). Articles by Dr. Billingsley have appeared in many professional publications, and he has testified on behalf of families before congressional committees.

Extended Family

HENRY H. MITCHELL, Ph.D.

Like many so-called primitive cultures and religions, the African world view is based on the extended family. I suppose all cultures begin with families and tribes (which are extended families), but the African experience never outgrew it. People in African cultural traditions still know no other way to relate to each other than in family terms and family feelings.

Southern whites picked up names like "Auntie" for black women to avoid calling them "missus," but it should be understood that in African languages there was no word for "missus." In an African community, every woman is mother, or aunt, or grandmother, or sister, or daughter. There is no title for a person whose respect and status is in any way to be dissociated from one's own family. When masters started calling these women "Auntie," it was because everybody else called them "Auntie." There was no such word as "missus" available, since in their world there were no nonrelatives.

"The Continuity of African Culture," Henry H. Mitchell, from *This Far by Faith*, copyright © 1977 The Liturgical Conference, 810 Rhode Island Avenue, N. E., Washington, D.C. 20018. Used with permission. All rights reserved.

Henry H. Mitchell, Ph.D., is the dean of the School of Theology at Virginia Union University in Richmond. He was the first Martin Luther King, Jr., memorial professor of Black Church studies at Colgate Rochester Divinity School/Bexley Hall Crozer Seminary in Rochester, New York. Director of the Ecumenical Center for Black Church studies in Los Angeles for eight years, he has held pastorates in California and is the author of *Black Preaching, Black Belief* and *The Recovery of Preaching* (Harper & Row).

Spiral of Family Relationships

Sr. THEA BOWMAN, FSPA, Ph.D.

Look at the top half of the Spiral of Family Relationships. Think of your own family. Don't just think of father, mother, and children, but think of your whole family—parents, grandparents, cousins, nieces, nephews, in-laws, outlaws, adopted relatives. Think of all the people related to you by blood and/or choice and commitment.

Now visualize them. How would you describe your family? Expectant parents? Old parents? Kissing cousins? Newly professed families? Loyal Catholics? Questioning Catholics? Confused Catholics?

Then look at the bottom half of the Spiral. How does or how can your family best accomplish the family functions indicated there: giving and supporting life, treasuring Black history and heritage, living Black values, worshiping the Lord, and challenging the Church to be truly Christian?

Discuss what it means to be family and what it means to be a Black family really diving into the treasures of our heritage. Discuss what it means to be a Black Catholic family, dedicated to the Church and witnessing that our religion is good, that it is meaningful to us, and really is Catholic people sharing the Good News of the Lord Jesus Christ within our communities.

Discuss how Black people in America survived because of family. How Black families gathered together in communities, sharing a common history; our African experience; the Middle Passage; slavery; our segregated experience in America; and the struggle for freedom, equality, and the recognition of our citizenship and human dignity.

Discuss how we share a common heritage, common ways of thinking and responding and expressing the life of the Spirit. Think of how our culture was developed by particular people in particular circumstances, embodying particular responses to what it meant to be family, doing Black things in Black ways.

Courtesy of Southern Cross

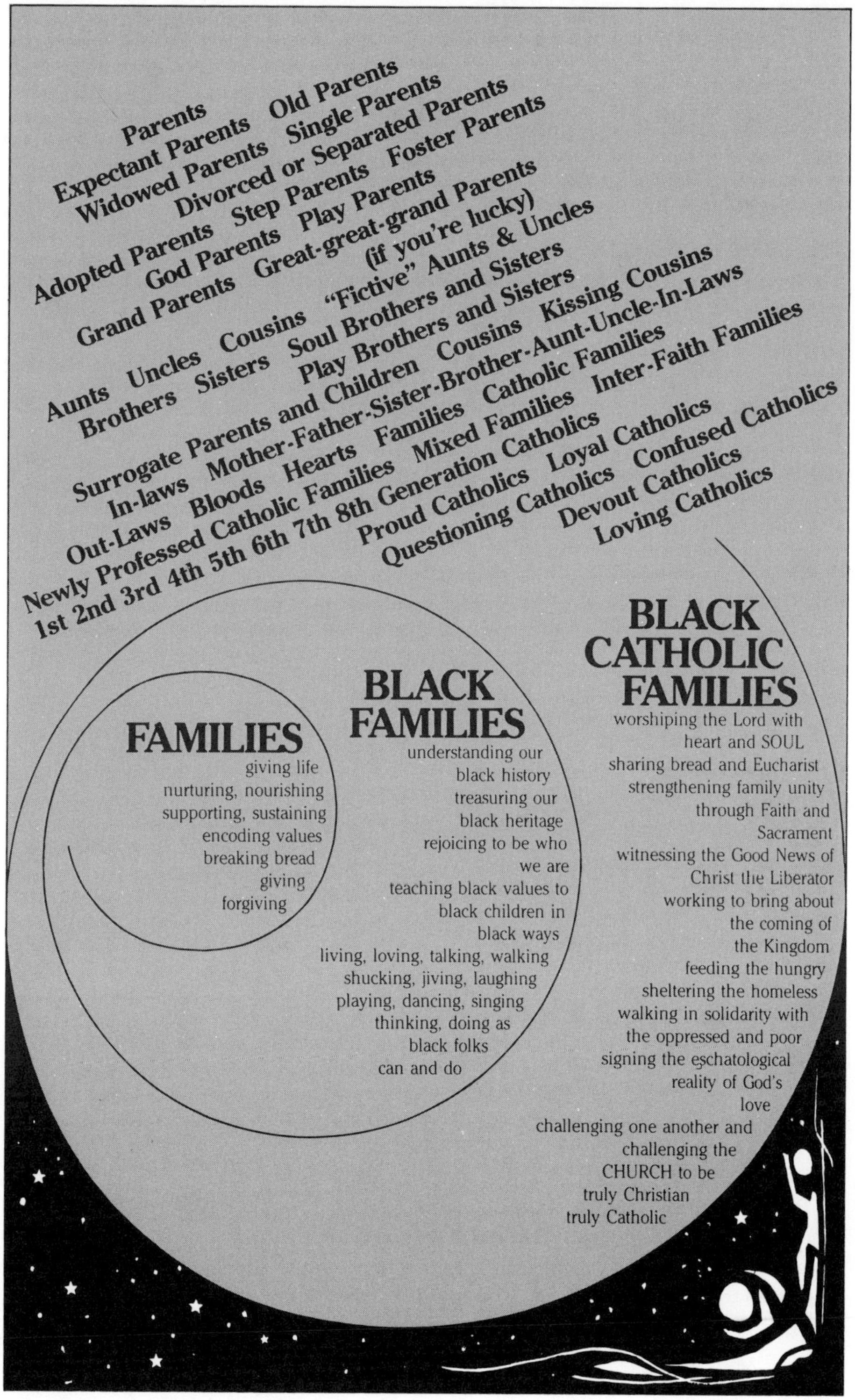

Parents Old Parents
Expectant Parents Single Parents
Widowed Parents Divorced or Separated Parents
Step Parents Foster Parents
Adopted Parents Play Parents
God Parents Great-great-grand Parents
(if you're lucky)
Grand Parents
Aunts Uncles Cousins "Fictive" Aunts & Uncles
Soul Brothers and Sisters
Brothers Sisters Play Brothers and Sisters
Cousins Kissing Cousins
Surrogate Parents and Children
In-laws Mother-Father-Sister-Brother-Aunt-Uncle-In-Laws
Catholic Families Inter-Faith Families
Out-Laws Bloods Hearts Families Mixed Families
Newly Professed Catholic Families
1st 2nd 3rd 4th 5th 6th 7th 8th Generation Catholics
Proud Catholics Loyal Catholics
Questioning Catholics Confused Catholics
Devout Catholics
Loving Catholics
FAMILIES
giving life
nurturing, nourishing
supporting, sustaining
encoding values
breaking bread
giving
forgiving
BLACK FAMILIES
understanding our
black history
treasuring our
black heritage
rejoicing to be who
we are
teaching black values to
black children in
black ways
living, loving, talking, walking
shucking, jiving, laughing
playing, dancing, singing
thinking, doing as
black folks
can and do
BLACK CATHOLIC FAMILIES
worshiping the Lord with
heart and SOUL
sharing bread and Eucharist
strengthening family unity
through Faith and
Sacrament
witnessing the Good News of
Christ the Liberator
working to bring about
the coming of
the Kingdom
feeding the hungry
sheltering the homeless
walking in solidarity with
the oppressed and poor
signing the eschatological
reality of God's
love
challenging one another and
challenging the
CHURCH to be
truly Christian
truly Catholic

You will be capable of bringing to the Catholic Church the precious and original contribution of "negritude" which she needs particularly in this historic hour.

Pope Paul VI
The Teachings of Pope Paul VI
Vatican: *Liberia Editrice Vaticana*, 1969

What Is Family?

ANDREW BILLINGSLEY, PH.D.

"Family" in the Black community is not confined to husband, wife, and children. There are many extensions of family that spread throughout the neighborhood and community.

EXTENDED FAMILIES

The types of extended families include: (a) the incipient extended family, consisting of a married couple with no children of their own, who take in other relatives; (b) the simple extended family, consisting of a married couple with their own children, who take in other relatives; and (c) the attenuated extended family, consisting of a single, abandoned, legally separated, divorced, or widowed mother or father living with his or her own children, who takes into the household other relatives. Each of these patterns exists in appreciable numbers among [Black] families.

There are four classes of relatives who can and often do come to live with [Black] families. These are (a) minor relatives, including grandchildren, nieces, nephews, cousins, and young siblings under eighteen; (b) peers of the primary parents, including, particularly, siblings, cousins, and other adult relatives; (c) elders of the primary parents, including, particularly, aunts and uncles; and finally, (d) parents of the primary family heads. The structure of authority, to mention only one aspect of family life, may shift considerably, depending on the status of the relative coming to live in the family.

There is a further basis for differentiating subtypes of extended families. Some relatives who come to live with a family come alone. They become, then, secondary members of the family. Other relatives come with their spouses or their children. These become subfamilies. There are, then, incipient subfamilies, or husband and wife pairs who come to live in the household of their relatives; simple nuclear subfamilies, consisting of husband, wife, and their small children, who live with another family; and attenuated subfamilies, consisting of one parent and his or her children, living in a relative's household. Furthermore, it is very common for two families of siblings or other relatives to share the same household.

AUGMENTED FAMILIES

These are families which have unrelated individuals living with them as roomers, boarders, lodgers, or other relatively long-term guests. Since these unrelated persons often exert major influence in the organization of [Black] families, this group of families is referred to collectively as *augmented* families.

SYNCRETIC FAMILIES

In these families, the leadership is shared. Decision making is participatory, and family members work together to achieve family goals.

Excerpted from *Black Families in White America*, Andrew Billingsley (Englewood-Cliffs, N.J.: Prentice-Hall, 1968).

Andrew Billingsley, Ph.D., is professor of sociology and Afro-American studies at the University of Maryland. A former president of Morgan State University in Baltimore, he was visiting scholar and professor of social welfare at the Institute for the Study of Social Change of the University of California, Berkeley. His extensive writing includes the influential *Black Families in White America* (Prentice-Hall), *Children of the Storm* (Harcourt, Brace) and *Black Families and the Struggle for Survival* (Friendship Press). Articles by Dr. Billingsley have appeared in many professional publications, and he has testified on behalf of families before congressional committees.

Where? How Many?

Fr. CYPRIAN DAVIS, OSB, Ph.D.

How large is the Catholic presence in the Black community? The answer is probably not very large. But the question perhaps could be phrased another way. How significant is the size of the Black Catholic community? Even more pertinent perhaps is the question of how significant is the size of the Black Catholic community in certain areas and in comparison with other significant Black religious communities.

The total Black population in the United States in the 1980 Census is 26 million people. In 1940, the Black population was 12 million.[1] According to recent estimates, the number of Black Catholics in the United States is 1,294,103.[2] This is four times the number in 1940, when Black Catholics were 300,000, or in 1975, when they reached a little less than a million.[3] Part of the increase in the number of Black Catholics in this country is in some measure due to the influx of Haitians in recent years. This fact has had significant impact on the growth of the Catholic Church in certain areas.

According to the Census of 1980, New York state has over 2 million Blacks and is the state with the largest Black population. It is not surprising then that the Diocese of Brooklyn has the largest number of Black Catholics: 110,000. Nevertheless, in terms of Black population centers, the largest numbers of Blacks are still to be found in the South Atlantic states; the next areas in density are the Middle Atlantic and the East North Central states. Second to Brooklyn in Black Catholic population centers is the Archdiocese of Chicago, with 100,000 Black Catholics; and third, the Archdiocese of New Orleans, with 90,500 Black Catholics.

This means that in the Brooklyn diocese, 8 out of every 100 Catholics are Black. It also means that in the New York area about 8 percent of the Black population is Catholic. In the Chicago area, 7 percent of the Black population is Catholic. And in the New Orleans archdiocese, 27 percent of the Black population is Catholic. Overall, with a United States Catholic population of 52,392,934 and a Black Catholic population of 1,294,103, this means that some 2 percent of the Catholic population is Black, while some 5 percent of the Black population today is Catholic.[4]

Although there are no hard figures, the national association of Black priests estimates that there are today about 300 Black priests, some 285 Black permanent deacons, and between 150 and 200 Black seminarians. There are also some 100 Black brothers and approximately 700 Black sisters. There are at present 10 Black bishops, one of whom is an ordinary, some 3 or 4 Black provincials, and 1 Black monsignor.[5]

It is even more difficult to ascertain the exact number of Black parishes since most parishes are to some extent integrated. In the urban areas, however, a large proportion of the student body in the Catholic schools is Black. As a result, it can be said that in many of the metropolitan areas throughout the country, but especially in the Mid-Atlantic states, the East North Central area, and the southern Louisiana area, the presence of Black Catholics and Black Catholic institutions is highly visible.

Black Catholics in relation to Black Protestant Churches are also highly visible. The largest Black Baptist denomination is the National Baptist Convention, U.S.A. The latest membership figures available indicate a membership of 6.82 million. The National Baptist Convention of America is somewhat smaller, with a membership of 3.5 million. The oldest Black Protestant denomination in the United States, The African Methodist Episcopal Church, has a membership of 3.25 million and the Church of God in Christ, a membership of 2.9 million. The next largest Black Protestant denomination is the African Methodist Episcopal Zion Church, with a membership of 1.2 million. Finally, the Progressive National Baptist Convention has a membership of 1 million and the Christian Methodist Episcopal Church numbers 800,000 communicants. These statistics represent the largest Black Churches.[6] Black communicants in other denomina-

CHD/Michal Heron

Fr. Cyprian Davis, OSB, Ph.D., Benedictine monk of St. Meinrad Archabbey in Indiana, is professor of church history at St. Meinrad School of Theology and author of a high school textbook on Church history. He has written articles on Black Catholic history and spirituality, and on monastic history. Fr. Davis serves as archivist for St. Meinrad Archabbey and for the National Black Catholic Clergy Caucus.

tions that are not all Black are not as numerous, with one exception. The 1,294,000 Black Catholics put the Catholic Church as fifth in membership among Black Churches. In this sense, the Black Catholic community is significant in terms of Black religion and Black religious experience.

NOTES

1. United States Bureau of the Census, Table no. 36, in *Statistical Abstract of the United States, 1982–1983* (Washington, D.C.: United States Bureau of the Census, 1982).

2. There are no current published figures. This information was conveyed by Fr. John J. Harfmann, SSJ, of the Josephite Pastoral Center, Washington, D.C.

3. George Shuster, SSJ, and Robert M. Kearns, SSJ, Table no. 3, "Dioceses Ranked by Change in Black Population: 1960–1970," in *Statistical Profile of Black Catholics* (Washington, D.C.: Josephite Pastoral Center, 1976), 13–15.

4. These figures for black Catholics were supplied by Fr. John J. Harfmann, SSJ. The statistics for the current Catholic population are given in the *Official Catholic Directory. 1984* (New York: P.J. Kenedy & Sons, 1984).

5. The information regarding the numbers of black priests, seminarians, deacons, and brothers was supplied by the National Black Catholic Clergy Caucus in Washington, D.C. The information regarding the number of black sisters was supplied by the National Black Sisters' Conference in Oakland, California.

6. Each religious denomination numbers its membership differently. Catholics count all those who are baptized. This is not the case everywhere. It is not very easy, moreover, to acquire exact numbers in many instances. The numbers cited in the article for the membership in black Churches was taken from an article entitled "Ten Religious Groups with Biggest Black Memberships," EBONY 39 (March 1984): 140–44. Upon inquiry, those Church leaders consulted agreed with the numbers presented in this article. The article points out that the Catholic Church is the fifth largest and that the United Methodist Church (which is also not a black Church) is the tenth largest with a black membership of 376,000.

Courtesy of the John Reese Family

Afro-American Families An Element of Actualization

HARRIETTE PIPES McADOO, PH.D.

One of the traditional and continuing stress-absorbing systems for Black families has been the wider supportive network of their families. These reciprocal exchange systems have enabled Blacks to cope with, and sometimes transcend, severe environmental stress. These networks extend beyond the house to include relatives of several generations. They often include friends and church members who become as family or *fictive kin*.

The extended family-help system, the "elasticity" of family boundaries, the high level of informal adoption, and the important supportive role of religious groups, have augmented existing internal family supports in being able to cope with stress. The wider extended families are a source of emotional and instrumental strength, especially during periods of high stress. The "kin insurance policies" were very active because goods and services flow in both directions between mobile and nonmobile family members.

CHD/Barbara Baker Stephenson

Families with more limited physical or economic resources do have greater problems. It is more difficult to raise children alone than with a spouse or with the help of relatives. It is more difficult to be poor and elderly than to be in the prime of life. Yet the number of adults in the home or the age of the family members does not limit the family in being able to care for its members. With the support provided by the support networks, families have maintained their function, independent of formal structure.

Children without homes have traditionally been adopted informally within the wider family, church, or even neighborhood. This was a continuation of the desire to keep children with kin and an extension of African-based beliefs that children belong to a wider clan, or family, and not just to one or two individuals. Until recently, social agencies preferred to take children from this network and place them in foster care with a series of strangers. The policies have only recently allowed support payments to be made to kin who care for children. Until then, families had to give up their young relative if the financial burdens became too heavy.

A similar pattern now exists with the care of the elderly. In Black families, there is a tabu against putting elderly family members in institutions to be cared for by strangers. Yet governmental policy forces the family to remove the frail elderly from the home in order to get help with expensive medical care. Many elderly do without in order to stay out of institutions.

The church can help augment the existing natural networks present in the community. Informal sharing groups can be organized on a neighborhood basis. Single-mother support groups can help with sharing emotional support and child-care needs. Cooperative food-buying plans can be church-based. Elderly members could be helped effectively to use resources that are available to all. All are means of actualizing family and church values within the Black community.

***Afro-American Families: An Element of Actualization*, Harriette Pipes McAdoo (unpublished) Paper delivered at the joint meeting of the National Black Sisters' Conference, National Black Catholic Clergy Caucus and National Black Catholic Seminarians' Association, Chicago (August 1980), copyright © 1980 National Black Catholic Clergy Caucus, Washington, D.C. Reprinted with permission.**

Harriette Pipes McAdoo, Ph.D., is acting dean of the School of Social Work at Howard University in Washington, D.C., where she is a professor in the research sequence. Editor of *Black Families* (Sage), she has published in the areas of family support networks, single parenting, ethnic families, and the development of self-esteem and racial attitudes in Black children.

Afro-American Families

PART II

The Challenge

Nobody will save us,
from us, for us,
but us.

Jesse Jackson

The Black Experience in a Western Church

EDWIN J. NICHOLS, Ph.D.

A review of the current literature on Black families indicates

- unemployment rates are up
- suicide rates are up
- murder of Black males rates are up
- alcoholism rates are up
- drug abuse rates are up
- school drop-outs are up
- teen-age pregnancy rates are up

With so many of the ills of society being up for Blacks in the country, the Black Catholic family is at a point of crisis. The Chinese character for the word crisis is composed of two figures:

One figure means *danger*; the other means *opportunity*.

While the family of this ethnic group is in the presence of danger, there is also the opportunity to survive and advance. The major opportunity for the Black Catholic family is to become the change agents to the Church and urban society. In order to become such a change agent, one must

1. establish the uniqueness of one's own identity,
2. analyze the mechanisms of the system that needs to be changed, and
3. set one's goals and objectives for that change.

Rogelio Solis/Courtesy of Mississippi Today

Edwin J. Nichols, Ph.D., chief of the Staff College of the National Institute of Mental Health, Rockville, Maryland, was a visiting professor at the University of Ibadan, Nigeria, where he directed the Child's Clinic. Educated in Canada and Germany, he received his Doctor of Philosophy cum laude from Leopol-Franz Universitat, Austria. He maintains a private clinical and industrial psychological practice.

THE CHALLENGES

stress
loneliness frustration worry
anxiety obsession oppression
repression depression bills inflation
insecurity poverty unemployment underemployment
layoffs rip-offs last-hired first-fired
injustice unequal opportunity
systematic exclusion from full participation in political,
social, educational, economic, and
religious organizations and institutions
inadequate education inadequate housing
homelessness inadequate health care
inadequate sanitation inadequate nutrition
retardation senility starvation aggression
violence crime murder rape robbery incest conflict
economic conflict religious conflict family conflict
crime black-on-black crime jail
imprisonment police brutality violence
family violence child abuse wife abuse husband abuse
teen-age pregnancies unwanted pregnancies
abortion frustration alcohol abuse drug abuse
chemical dependency illness accident hypochondria
dependency agency dependency delinquency
street gangs rumbles wars
drop-outs cop-outs run-aways
hustlers dealers pimping
prostitution
separation death suicide
mobility upward mobility
materialism consumerism
elitism classism racism sexism
manipulation exploitation
anxiety loneliness
stress

Black Christian Perspective of Spirituality

FR. ALBERT M. MCKNIGHT, CSSP

Black people today in the United States are in a Great Black Depression. They are economically depressed with an official unemployment rate of 13 percent, but unofficially, 20 percent. Our teen-age unemployment runs as high as 50 percent in many of our urban centers and 80 percent in rural areas. But what is far worse—Black People are spiritually depressed. There is a great depression of the Black Spirit. We seem to be losing "soul." There are signs of social disintegration all around us. Here are some disturbing statistics: One of every two Black marriages is ending in divorce; the number one killer of Blacks today is murder by other Blacks. There is a frightening increase of Black on Black crimes. And, there is the skyrocketing suicide rate among Blacks. Ten years ago, a Black killing himself was unheard of, and yet the group with the highest suicide rate in the country today is young Black males between the ages of fifteen and twenty-five. The use of drugs is at the crisis stage in our communities. Mental illness is increasing. Our youngsters are dropping out of school at an alarming rate, and our high schools are graduating illiterates.

A genuine spirituality for Black people living in racist, capitalistic U.S.A. involves the struggle of putting on the Lord Jesus Christ within the context of the spiritual and physical violence which has been and continues to be an integral part of the Black experience in the United States.

Black Spirituality must be developed out of the context of what white racist U.S.A. has done to us. We need a Black Spirituality which would help us to struggle against the dehumanizing oppression and expoitation of this society.

As Albert Cleage has so poignantly written, "Black people in America have been programmed for inferiority deliberately, consistently, exquisitely." The white man's declaration of Black inferiority is basic to all American life. There is no institution in America, no aspect of American life that does not basically reflect the declared inferiority of all Black people. Not poor Black people, not ignorant Black people, not uncouth Black people, but all Black people have been declared inferior. This declaration of Black inferiority is the foundation on which American history has been built. From the time Black people were brought to these shores as slaves, the declaration of Black inferiority was the framework within which the Black man was forced to build his existence. In the slave ship, on the slave block, on the plantation, fleeing from the lynch mob, fleeing north into slum ghettos, the Black man was not only declared inferior, but everything possible was done to make that declaration a statement of fact. The Black man could accept this declaration of inferiority, or he could reject it; and for the early part of his existence in America, the Black man accepted the white man's declaration of Black inferiority. As a slave, systematically separated from people who spoke his language, living in a country about which he knew nothing, not even the simple geography necessary to attempt his escape, he was forced to accept the authority of the white slave master to define his person and the conditions of his existence.

CHD/Michal Heron

There is no Blackness without struggle. Struggle is central to the Black experience. We must struggle against those who oppress and exploit us, but more important, we must struggle against our own internal weaknesses. We must struggle against our own lack of clarity and lack of discipline. We must struggle to take the time to investigate, identify, and institutionalize our own nature and principles of development and defense. We must struggle to work hard and sacrifice for what we need and see this struggle as a spiritual process of putting on the Lord Jesus Christ. Putting on the Lord Jesus Christ for us means dying to the nigger mentality and rising to the new person, the African personality. We must die to European values of individualism, dog-eat-dog competition, materialistic consumerism, and anything for money.

Fr. Albert M. McKnight, CSSp, is pastor of Holy Ghost Church in Opelousas, Louisiana. He serves as president of the Southern Cooperative Development Fund, vice-chairperson of the National Consumer Coop Bank, and chairperson of the Consumer Cooperative Development Corporation, all headquartered in Lafayette, Louisiana.

Lerone Bennett has said that Blackness is a challenge. Blackness is a challenge because it raises the whole question of values and because it tells us that we must rise now to the level of teaching this profoundly ignorant and profoundly sick society. And in order to do that we must create a rationale. We must create a new rationality, a new way of seeing, a new way of reasoning, a new way of thinking. Our present way of thinking, and the scholarship which undergirds that way of thinking, is European-centered. It is property and place-centered, not people-oriented. We see now through a glass whitely, and there can be no more desperate and dangerous task than the task which faces us now, of trying to see with our eyes, trying to see through a glass blackly. Our way of thinking must become African. It must become people-oriented. Only through struggle shall we establish our identity. Only through struggle shall we establish our purpose. Only through struggle shall we establish our direction. Through struggle we must rise to the new person, the African personality with new values; namely, the values of unity, self-determination, collective work and responsibility, familyhood and cooperative economics, purpose, creativity, and faith; in other words, the Nguzo Saba.

CHD/Michal Heron

White Christianity and white theology have been so concerned about orthodoxy (i.e., the right kind of teaching) that they have grossly neglected "ortho-practice," the right kind of practice. Black Spirituality and Black theology must be concerned with the process of developing ortho-practice, the right kind of practice (i.e., a life style which helps us to be in action the people of God). Black Spirituality must be wholistic, for holiness is nothing but wholeness. We cannot be holy without being a whole person. Wholeness involves loving oneself and one's people. Wholeness involves acting for oneself and one's community. Holiness involves being concerned about all aspects of life. Therefore, Black Spirituality must involve the whole person embracing all aspects of Black life. We must learn to pray as if everything depended upon God and work in all aspects of life as if everything depended upon ourselves.

Black Spirituality must encompass psychology, politics, and education. Black Spirituality must encompass economics and morals, and through the dialectical process of struggling in all areas of Black life, the new person, the true African personality will be developed and Jesus Christ will be lived. . . .

We must know that we are all African people. We are genetically African because our ancestors are African. We are historically African because our history is one with that of other African people—an oppressed and exploited people. We are culturally African because everything we control (e.g., our music, the Black Church, our art, etc.) expresses the African personality distinct from all other cultures.

We have both strengths and weaknesses, and we must learn to struggle to maximize our strengths and minimize our weaknesses.

To grow in the spirit, we must be able to assume responsibility for our ideas and feelings and strive towards self-actualization, engaging in cooperative interactions, and having the capacity for intimate and personal relationships. We must develop interpersonal skills so that we can effectively develop intimate and personal relationships with each other, for the mystery of self-knowledge is that only in relating to some other person on a meaningful level can one get to know oneself. To initiate, develop, and maintain effective and fulfilling relationships, certain basic skills must be present. These skills generally fall into four areas: (1) knowing and trusting each other; (2) accurately and unambiguously understanding each other; (3) influencing and helping each other; and (4) constructively resolving problems and conflicts in one's relationship.

To become normal, we must know our purpose in life. At this particular period in history, according to the signs of the times, our most sacred purpose must be to struggle for the unification, liberation, and independence of all people, but primarily those of African descent and primarily those where we live.

First, we must struggle for unity because we know that if we do not learn to unify (i.e., work together), we will contribute to our own destruction. If, instead of unifying, we continue our individualism (doing our own thing), we can have no liberation or independence. Instead, we will have slavery and dependency.

We must struggle for unity on three different levels. The first level of unity is with ourselves. We must know with our whole being that we are somebody, that we are the most important persons in the world, that we are the greatest miracles in the world. We must love ourselves and be one with ourselves—with our bodies, minds, and spirits all going in the same direction. In other words we must be "together persons."

The second level of struggle for unity must be within the family, within the same household. Husbands and wives must struggle with each other to establish oneness. Parents and children must struggle with one another so that the family will be the school and the social center of unity.

The third level of struggle for unity is within the wider community; but only when there is struggle on the first and second levels will the struggle for unity within the wider community be successful.

The struggle for unity within the family and wider community succeeds when those involved commit themselves to practice in their relationships with each other the group norms of trust, honesty, openness, liberation, acceptance, understanding, support, communication, sharing, feelings, feedback, risk taking, responsibility, respect, and staying in the present (here and now).

Second, we must struggle for liberation, which is the process of struggling to become that unique person whom God made us to be. We must struggle against external domination and our own internal contradictions. Without freedom, we will remain slaves of another people and victims of our own weaknesses.

Third, we must struggle for independence, which is the perfection of freedom. The highest form of independence is self-reliance, which is the ability to do for oneself while being willing to help others and be helped by them.

"Black Christian Perspective of Spirituality," Albert M. McKnight, CSSp, from *Theology: A Portrait in Black,* Thaddeus J. Posey, OFM Cap., editor, copyright © 1980 National Black Catholic Clergy Caucus, Washington, D.C. Reprinted with permission.

CHD/Peter Magubane

Abortion, Poverty and Black Genocide: Gifts to the Poor?

ERMA CLARDY CRAVEN

I am somebody. . . .
I can see, I can hear, I can feel, I can touch! . . .
I am—
Jesse Jackson

Throughout the course of American history, the quality of human life has always been improved at the expense of the weak and oppressed. The tragic awareness of this reality leads one to the inexorable conclusion that the quality of life has never been a universally applied concept. This has never been so true as it is today in the move toward human abortion. It takes little imagination to see that the unborn Black baby is the real object of many abortionists. Except for the privilege of aborting herself, the Black woman and her family must fight for every other social and economic privilege. This move toward the free application of a nonright (abortion) for those whose real need is equal human rights and opportunities is benumbing the social conscience of America into unquestioningly accepting the "smoke screen" of abortion. The quality of life for the poor, the Black, and the oppressed will not be served by destroying their children.

Held in bondage for decades, the Black man served the master society. His humanness was ruled out of existence by the law and social "norms." His only function was to advance the slave owners' prestige and economic gain. Every effort was made to destroy the Black family; knowing that with its destruction, the Black man remained powerless. But we hung on, and in the 1960s, civil rights legislation brought some equality to those who were already equal. While all seemed good and power seemed imminent, the plight of the Black man, woman, and child did not improve, but only changed from the plantation to the ghetto; and the chains of slavery took on newer, more subtle and sophisticated forms. Prejudice and poverty now kept the Black family in a powerless state. Now, the womb of the Black woman is seen as the latest battleground for oppression. In times past, the Blacks couldn't grow kids fast enough for their "masters" to harvest; now that power is near, the "masters" want us to call a moratorium on having babies. When looked at in context, the whole mess adds up to blatant genocide.

Courtesy of the John Reese Family

"Abortion, Poverty and Black Genocide: Gifts to the Poor?" Erma Clardy Craven, from *Abortion and Social Justice*, Dennis J. Horan and Thomas W. Hilgers, editors, Kansas City, Ks.: Sheed & Ward, Inc. Copyright © 1972 by Dennis J. Horan. Reprinted with permission.

Erma Clardy Craven is a social worker with extensive professional experience in social agencies in both Minneapolis and New York City. The founder of Minnesota Pro-Life Social Workers, Ms. Craven is active on the boards of many Minnesota pro-life organizations. She has given lectures and workshops on Right to Life issues in twenty states and Great Britain.

It Is Not Sufficient that We Fight against Abortion

BISHOP JAMES P. LYKE, OFM, PH.D.

In January 1981, an estimated 65,000 marchers made their way to the nation's capital to protest the killing of fetal life and to strengthen the move for a human life amendment to the Constitution. Reagan's Health and Human Services secretary, Richard S. Schweiker delivered a heartening address to the throng. "You know very well," he said, "that you have a friend in the Health and Human Services Department of the Reagan administration."

The subversive, January 22, 1973, decision of the Supreme Court must be overturned. Law has both an educative and determinative function: by its very force, law affirms and communicates a value and regulates human behavior. One cannot be *pro-choice* and personally against abortion. Such a position reduces one's conviction about abortion to the level of secondary values and ignores the inherent power of law. Were I to suggest that we institute a pro-choice movement regarding freedom and racial justice, one would assume that, however much I might *personally* support these values, they obviously do not prioritize highly in my personal value system since I readily make their existence a matter of individual choice. Surely, democracy (communal choice) and individual choice are built on human rights, not vice versa. We do not vote on "life, liberty, and the pursuit of happiness." These values are nondebatable precisely because they come from God and form the ontological base for human existence. It is imperative, therefore, that human law confirm on earth what has already been written in heaven:

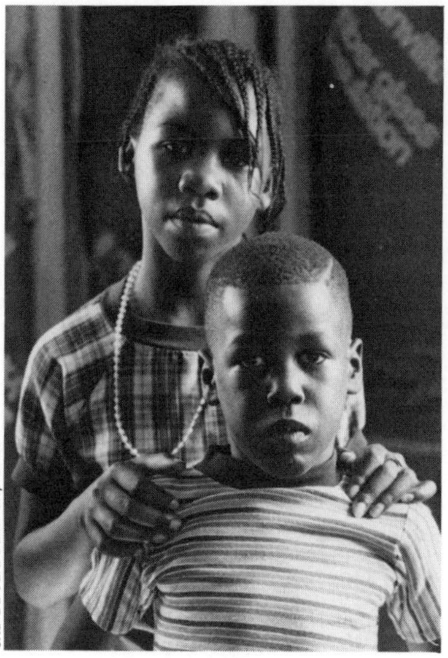

CHD/Barbara Baker Stephenson

Truly you have formed my inmost being;
you knit me in my mother's womb.
I give you thanks that I am so fearfully, wonderfully made;
wonderful are your works.
My soul also you knew full well;
nor was my frame unknown to you
When I was made in secret,
when I was fashioned in the depths of the earth.

Psalm 139:13–15

It is not sufficient, however, that we fight against abortion. It is far more important that we be pro-life in behalf of the very existence of the child as well as the quality of life for the child and mother after birth. The pregnant mother must not be left alone in a state of inner turmoil and conflict. Assurance for both child and mother is offered by such organizations as Birthright, Womankind, and Catholic Family and Children Services.

I have not entered the biological, psychological, or sociological debates that revolve around the morality of abortion. Even the most rabid pro-abortionist, however, will acknowledge that the arguments in behalf of abortion do not lend to absolute certitude. Given the fact that "life" is a fundamental, bedrock value (there is no "liberty and pursuit of happiness" without life), I would argue that one must always have a preferential option for life! In the words of the noted Lutheran theologian, Dietrich Bonhoeffer: To raise the question whether we are here concerned already with a human being or not is merely to confuse the issue. The simple fact is that God certainly intended to create a human being.

Bishop James P. Lyke, OFM, Ph.D., became auxiliary bishop of the Diocese of Cleveland in 1979. Prior to that he was a parish priest and pastor at St. Benedict the Black Church in Grambling, Louisiana and St. Thomas Church in Memphis. He was also director of the Newman Center in Grambling. Author of the filmstrip *Black Married Love,* published by the National Office for Black Catholics, Bishop Lyke developed programs for engaged couples in the churches he served.

In an aside, let me conclude by expressing a word of appreciation to President Reagan for his forceful and unequivocal stand for the humanity of fetal life. It is my prayer that he will defend the rights of the already born with equal passion.

"It Is Not Sufficient that We Fight against Abortion," Bishop James P. Lyke, OFM, originally published in THE CALL AND POST (Cleveland) copyright © February 21, 1981. Used with permission.

Rogelio Solis/Courtesy of Mississippi Today

The family is the fundamental human community; it is the first and vital cell of any society. Thus the strength and vitality of any country will only be as great as the strength and vitality of the family within that country. No group has a greater impact on a country than the family. No group has a more influential role in the future of the world.

Beloved brothers and sisters: all the families that make up the Church and all the individuals that make up the families, all of us together are called to walk with Christ, bearing witness to his truth in the circumstances of our daily lives. In doing this, we can permeate society with the leaven of the Gospel, which alone can transform it into Christ's kingdom—a kingdom of truth and life, a kingdom of holiness and grace, a kingdom of justice, love, and peace! Amen.

Pope John Paul II
Kenya, 1980

Sexuality and the Black Catholic Family An Interview with Dr. Edwin J. Nichols

CONDUCTED BY SR. THEA BOWMAN, FSPA

Sr. Thea: Dr. Nichols, from your perspective as a clinical and industrial psychologist, how do you see the contemporary black Catholic family?

Dr. Nichols: Well, the black Catholic family, like many families in our time, is in a state of crisis. If you look at the Chinese calligraphy for crisis, you see two figures, (1) Danger, and (2) Opportunity. At this juncture, we realize the dangerous situation in which the black Catholic family finds itself, but also we have an opportunity to survive and triumph over the times in which we live.

Sr. Thea: Given your schema, how do black people see themselves as sexual beings?

Dr. Nichols: I see black people as axiologically different from Europeans. From my perspective, Europeans have an axiology of person-to-the-object, which says that the highest value lies in the object or in the acquisition of the object. Black people have an axiology of person-to-person, which says the highest value lies in the meaningful interpersonal relationship. If you approach human sexuality from this perspective, then you can see quite readily why white women on many occasions say, "Don't treat me as a sex object." But, within black families and with black situations, that would not be a viable remark, because sexual relations, to blacks, are a mutual relation rather than something done to someone. If you listen to our music you will find that our songs express this idea of something that is done mutually, with great joy, great fervor, and great skill, as opposed to an accommodation, as opposed to being acted upon.

Rogelio Solis/Courtesy of Mississippi Today

Sr. Thea: Are patterns of family relationship in black culture radically different from those in other cultures?

Dr. Nichols: Yes. Black families still function with strong kinship bonds. Kin can mean persons who are not blood related. Blacks, for example, may have an Aunt Mary or an Uncle Henry or someone like that to whom they owe reverence and respect, from whom they receive love and affection. A social worker might go into that environment and ask, "Is this your maternal or paternal relative?" The answer would be "neither." Outsiders are very perplexed; they don't understand that you can have someone who you are calling Aunt or Uncle when, in reality, there is no blood bond or kinship. But this is a very common phenomenon in black families. This Aunt or Uncle has the capacity to discipline children, and by the same token, is the person who will feed you when your mother is not there—or clothe, or bathe you, or whatever is necessary to nurture you because this is a part of that black axiology of person-to-person, and your community is responsible for your nurture and growth development.

At a time when most research on black families concentrated on negatives, Robert Hill, in a seminal work, *The Strengths of Black Families*, named and statistically verified these strengths. He showed how strong kinship bonds have helped black families maintain health and wholeness in really adverse circumstances.

Another point that is significant is that black husbands and wives function on an egalitarian basis; there is a sharing of the responsibility for work and also for child rearing that you probably do not have in other families. A third factor is the extended family. Relatives—cousins, nieces, nephews—may one morning appear at your door; you have an obligation to your extended family to take them in, to support them, to care for them, pay their school fees, etc. Sometimes they get into trouble with their own families, or in the city, and they have to come as a predelinquent practically; but they are sent to you for you to be responsible for them, and that is seen as a part of your responsibility, and you accept it and do it quite openly and freely. To corroborate that, I think you need to look at a work by Dr. Harriette Pipes McAdoo, of Howard University. Her extensive research with middle-class black families in predominantly white communities shows that these patterns are still operative and functional.

Sr. Thea: Are sexual roles in black culture really radically different from those in other cultures?

Rogelio Solis/Courtesy of Mississippi Today

Dr. Nichols: In black culture, the concept of sexual role is best described as function not gender-specific; that is, black couples are basically egalitarian in their approach to function in the household. In European society, the role of the man is to work outside the home, and that's his job environment. When he comes home, things are prepared for him, and he is served as master of the household. There are jobs that are specifically women's jobs and jobs that are specifically men's.

Well, that's not a part of the black experience in this country. Within the household, black men function in any task that may be required. Ask black men if they can cook, wash clothes, scrub floors, clean the bathroom, any of those tasks, and 90 percent of them can and do.

Sr. Thea: What are the implications of all this for black Catholic families?

Dr. Nichols: Some black Catholic families have had a problem trying to define the essence of their Catholicism or religion. They postulate that the essence of Catholicism is greater than the essence of their blackness. They perceive their blackness to be a philosophical accident. Another group says, "By the grace of God, as a black family, we are Catholic." So the Catholicism is an integral part of the black family. The other group (in opposition) says, "We are a Catholic family, and just because of this philosophical accident we're black." When we try to get some parishes to work together, this can become a major problem. Black Catholics see themselves as Catholic first, black second.

Sr. Thea: Are you contrasting "I'm a Catholic who happens to be black" and "I'm a black who happens to be Catholic"?

Dr. Nichols: Now, historically, we have figured that we're Catholics. Yet we've been consistently required to come to terms with the way significant others—which means the white Catholic Church—saw us. Look at Mother Marie Theresa Maxis Duchemin, foundress of the Sisters and Servants of the Immaculate Heart of Mary. She was their first mother superior and helped to organize their value system. When she left the Oblate Sisters of Providence, in Baltimore, she went out to Monroe, Michigan. A very fair-skinned black woman, speaking French, Latin, etc., she assumed that she was being accepted as Catholic. When she arrived, she had to deal with racism, and, after a short while, she asked another nun not to join them because she was too dark complexioned. Now, this woman saw herself as Catholic. White "Christianity" saw her as just another black person, and therefore she was not able to do all of the things that she would have wanted to do in her order. She ended up in exile in Canada, and finally, as a broken woman, dying in one of her congregations.

By the same token, a priest, Patrick Healy, saw himself as a Catholic who was accidentally black, but more as a Jesuit, ordained in Paris, French educated, with an Irish father. He helped build Georgetown and made it into a viable and reputable university with standards from European universities. Then, when white Christianity, those contributors to funds for development of Georgetown University, came to the realization that he was a mulatto, their racism defined him. I'm saying that while we may see ourselves as Catholics who are black, others see us and say, "Oh, here come the black Catholics." So, unless we are able to accept that reality or redefine ourselves, we can have many problems trying to relate to the white "Christianity" that we find in the Catholic Church of this country at this time. It is a serious problem. The bishops themselves have come out with a letter discussing racism in the Church.

Sr. Thea: What are the implications of the black concept of sexual roles for the black Catholic family?

Dr. Nichols: Human sexuality is an integral part of being black. Intimacy is an integral part of being black. You cannot raise children with our child-rearing practices—a lot of touch, holding, nurturing, closeness—and then expect them to come to puberty or into contact in a social setting, male or female, and become neuters. We carry with us our capacity to touch and to be touched. We carry with us our capacity for intimacy and closeness. However, as black Catholics, we have constraints in our sexuality and prohibitions, in terms of conjugal kinds of expression. Therefore, to see young blacks holding, touching, dancing, being close is a part of the culture. One must not assume that this kind of behavior automatically means conjugal-genital consequences.

Sr. Thea: How do we open channels of communications so that when our children have serious concerns they will come to us?

Dr. Nichols: You have to start very early. You have to start having children tell it all. Coming from school, show and tell; coming from play, show and tell. You have to have the patience to sit down and listen to what they talk about. If you have not had the relationship of discussing everything with them, you will have to use your intuition. When you can see that something is wrong, stop. Say, "What's wrong?" They will tell you, "Oh, nothing." But you have to listen to "Oh, nothing," and let them talk about "Oh, nothing." You have to listen to "nothing" long enough to get a clue about what's going on. Don't pretend you haven't heard it or you don't want to hear it; but overtly suggest, "Is there something sexual going on that you aren't comfortable with?" The child may be surprised that you might consider that something sexual could be going on. Then you can say, "Oh, yes, these things happen. And if something has happened that's involving you, I think we need to talk about it." Do this in such a way that children are not ashamed or frightened or neurotic about their sexuality but, rather, accept the responsibilities and constraints and prohibitions against conjugal relationships within the framework of Catholicism.

Sr. Thea: Do you imply that it is true that black people tend to be more tactile, more sensual, perhaps more sexual than other people?

Dr. Nichols: Well, sexual in a positive way, yes, Tactile, and all these other things, yes, much more so than people who have an axiology of person-to-object, which says, if I touch you, I'm touching you for some reason. It is to acquire some object, and, therefore, the touch is the first stage in a rapid advance to some kind of conjugal relationship. But, in black communities, to touch, to hold, to embrace, to be near, to sit almost lap-to-lap on top of one another, does not of necessity mean that you are going to go immediately to some kind of conjugal relationship. In a person-to-person situation, you can be close to people and very warm and responsive; but, if that little spark that indicates sexuality or conjugal relationships is not there, then two people might as well sleep in the same room, because a sexual relationship is not going to take place. Now, this doesn't mean that we don't guard and protect our children (because they are young and spontaneous) from situations that could become conjugal, but that's not what every closeness means. I think that those are essential things to look at.

Sr. Thea: Without making them fearful, guilt-ridden, and anxious, how can we teach our children wholesome Christian values and how can we help them to grow into a sexuality that is responsible as well as life-giving?

Dr. Nichols: Start when the child is very young, by imprinting your values. If fidelity is your value, and your child grows up in a home where mother and father respect each other, where they can be close with friends and relatives and others who visit their homes, where they are really expressive in loving and holding, and where there's never a question of lack of fidelity between husband and wife; then the children will grow up seeing, feeling, and understanding fidelity as a value. It means you can have many friends and can be close to them, but you certainly don't have to be intimate in a sexual way. That is very important to teach both little boys and girls.

The other thing is to teach them self-respect. Tell them that when you share something as intimate as a human sexual relationship, you certainly don't share it with a wide range of people. Unless it represents deep caring, it loses all its dignity and spiritual quality. It becomes base and common, and it loses the true meaning within Christianity. With small children, your example, I think, is the most important thing with which to begin.

Then, be very specific in terms of the biology of sexuality. Children have to know all the parts of the body and how they function, and they have to know early. They need to understand their own sexual growth. Let me give you an example: We lived a mile from a Catholic high school. On that mile road, there was no bus transportation, so the boys hitchhiked to a place where they could get a bus. We had new neighbors, and one day we were all talking together. The son was a big sixteen-year-old, probably 6 ft., 2 in. tall. He looked much older. He said he was going to be hitchhiking.

I said, "Well, one of these times you're going to get in the car and somebody is going to say, "Oh, you certainly are a nice looking young man. Do you go to school nearby? Oh, you are so smart. Oh, what are you studying there?" Then, all of a sudden, you are going to feel his hand on your knee, on your leg, and in your crotch.

I thought my wife would die. She was so shocked that I would say something like this and tried to apologize for me in the presence of his parents, who had become very quiet. They had trusted me. I said, "Well, you know that's going to be that man's problem, not your problem." Then, I said, "What you should do is take his hand very firmly, hold it, and put it back on his lap. Then say, "Let me out, please!"

Well, my wife fussed at me after the company left. She was shocked. In less than six months, the boy came over to me and said, "You know, Dr. Nichols, you know what you told me? Well, it happened. But I didn't do what you said to do." I asked, "What did you do?" He said, "When he let me out, I hit him." I told the boy it was not necessary to hit. "Just get out of the car and don't bother him." But, the boy had been very angry. And, of course, he didn't come away thinking there was anything wrong with him, that he was a latent homosexual, or anything like that. It was that man's problem, and the boy got out of the car.

An openness is necessary. If you can't do it, maybe you can rely on someone, in that kinship network or extended family, who is open and can talk about things very candidly.

Sr. Thea: How can we teach children the kinds of values we hope they will grow into?

Dr. Nichols: Make a time every day when you talk with your children. Let them ramble and talk and say whatever they want to. Discuss what's going on. Share. That time should be about the same time every day. If somebody in the community gets pregnant, talk about what it means to be pregnant; talk about what she might have done to prevent the pregnancy and what you think will ultimately happen to her. Will this affect her education? Does she have to drop out of school? Does she have to try to raise this child? Will she have an abortion? Will she give the child up for adoption? Bring up all the issues. State your own personal values. Use events as they occur. If someone gets a divorce, discuss what that means during your talk time. One of my daughter's girlfriend's parents divorced, and for the first time I had some realization of how much anxiety our children had about divorce and how traumatic it was for them when another couple divorced. "What would happen to us if you divorced?" I use the events as they occur and discuss them.

Sr. Thea: You talked about the patterns of family relationship that are unique to black culture. What are some implications of that kind of family relationship for the black Catholic family?

Dr. Nichols: If you look at the black Church, not the black Catholic Church, you see that the extended family, the kinship, all of these behaviors are operative within the black Church. They are nurtured and supported within that framework, basically because the directors and leaders of the black Church are black people—black pastors, black choirmasters, black deacons, black trustees, etc. You also see egalitarian relationships within the black Church (a black woman in the pulpit, black women as trustees, deacons, etc.). Programs of the black Church corroborate, reinforce, and sustain black family values. Now black people are trying to bring their cultural values into the Catholic Church. It is very difficult in that structure to have black families' cultural values validated.

Sr. Thea: It has come to my attention that people in positions of trust have sometimes solicited black youths for sexual purposes. How can we protect our children from that kind of experience?

Dr. Nichols: I'm aware that we're speaking about some very specific situations in which trusted people who are homosexuals have solicited young blacks. In a situation like that, you have several responsibilities. You have one responsibility to prevent scandal. If you have evidence of this kind of behavior, let a person in authority know that you want this condition corrected. That's one level.

But my concern is less with the trusted person and his problem and more with the damage done to the child. If you are young and naive and don't know that these kinds of things go on, and someone who you idealize suddenly starts to fondle you in a sexual way, you probably wonder what is wrong with you. Perhaps you conclude that you are homosexual. The child may value the attention, but when he becomes more sophisticated he's angry, hostile, and bitter. He may lose his respect for people in authority because of the bad experience. If you get a vibe that things aren't what they should be, when your little bright-eyed boy comes running in and says "Oh, Mr. So-and-So is going to help me with my homework," say, "That's fine, I'll go with you," or "Your big brother is going with you, and he is going to sit there and listen while Mr. So-and-So helps you with your homework." That situation may happen once or twice, and he won't ask the child back.

If the child's a little older and more sophisticated, tease him in front of all the family and say, "You go on over there, but don't you let Mr. So-and-So kiss you now." Everybody laughs and a message is transmitted to the family that perhaps Mr. So-and-So has a problem. It is fine to relate to him, but when he wants to kiss you, it's time for you to come home. Children understand that, and they are prepared if an advance is made.

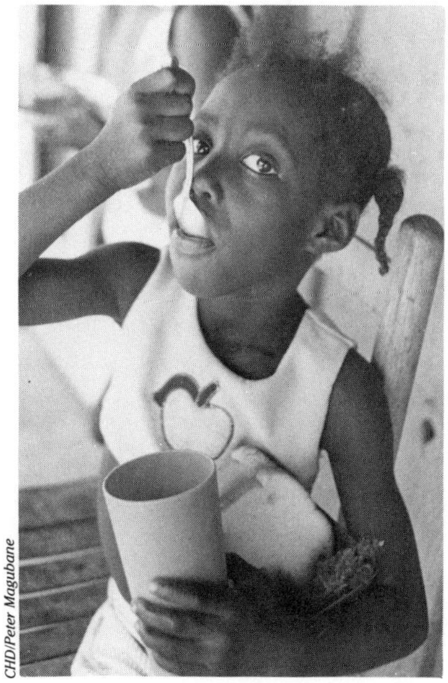

CHD/Peter Magubane

There are heterosexual situations that are equally as traumatic for the child. Girls of thirteen or fourteen can be all excited about some significant man in their lives. They are little girls in spite of the fact that they look like young women. They still sit on laps and embrace, particularly with figures with whom they feel safe. They are not conscious of their physical development or the possibility of stimulating other people sexually. And then to their astonishment, while hugging somebody, an erection suddenly comes between them and scares them half to death. Or somebody begins to feel or pat them. You have to help young girls in their exuberance, to realize that they are becoming young women and, that men are men. I tease them and say, "All right now, keep grabbing, hugging, and pulling on people. All of a sudden, somebody is going to pinch you or pat you. What are you going to do about that?" That's just enough warning, not to make the child guilty, but simply to suggest that some behaviors are more appropriate than others in such situations.

Sr. Thea: Recently, a lot of media attention has been given to the topic of incest.

Dr. Nichols: Incest has occurred throughout history. We are aware of this, but it is just becoming a topic for discussion. Formal research addressing incest in the black family is just beginning to be developed. A major study is currently under way at Children's Hospital in Washington, D.C.

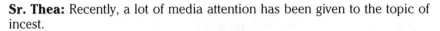

CHD/Peter Magubane

When I talk about incest, I like to distinguish four areas of concern which, in the effort to gather statistical data, are often lumped together: (1) father-daughter, mother-son incest; (2) incest between siblings; (3) incest involving other relatives; (4) other cases often statistically labeled father-daughter incest, but which I think are more properly labeled sexual assault.

First, father-daughter incest. In my clinical experience, I have known of incest between the natural father and daughter in white families. I have not encountered that in black families. I have encountered cases involving uncles or some other relatives, but not the natural father. This does not say it does not occur. It says the frequency is not very great. Incest between the natural father and the daughter rarely occurs in black families. Mother-son incest in black families is even more rare.

The highest incidence of incest in black families occurs between siblings—an older brother with a younger sibling, either male or female. Children are particularly vulnerable. When children share close quarters, close touching and fondling, some sexual play, some mutual masturbation, other forms of exploratory behavior, and in some instances actual penetration, can occur. These are things we have to guard against.

There are also times when incest involves cousins or uncles or other relatives. These cases are true incest. They raise very traumatic issues. It is difficult because people become involved in guilt and shame. They are afraid the police will come and take the father or the relative away. People are sworn to secrecy.

Again, I think if there is an openness and a capacity for children to discuss matters with their parents or with a favorite person in that kinship network, these things can come out, and proper intervention can be implemented.

Finally, there is the whole category that I call sexual assault. The stepfather or the mother's boyfriend or some other father figure engages in a sexual relationship with a thirteen or fourteen-year-old girl. The dynamic sometimes suggests that the mother is clinging to a younger boyfriend. She may feel threatened and may permit the behavior to continue. Or she may be angered with the attention the daughter is getting and project the blame. It's the daughter's problem. She was seductive to the man and what happened to her is her own fault.

Other issues of sexual assault occur when you have a young girl of seven or eight and boys in the community who are in early adolescence. They will sometimes catch a girl in a garage or someplace and sexually assault her, not rape in the true sense, but buy her candy or something like that, and then engage in exploratory behavior.

Sr. Thea: What can parents do in these situations?

Dr. Nichols: You have to be aware that these things occur. That's most important. Second, with that awareness, you have to be vigilant and talk openly about what occurs in the community or the neighborhood. Children are often sworn to secrecy on these subjects. You have to let them know there are different levels of secrecy. Sometimes they have secrets they don't tell others, but there are very few secrets that they can't tell their parents. They have to understand that someone who forces them to keep secrets is manipulating them. This person is not really interested in them and in having them keep a secret, but is preventing them from telling something that they are very ashamed of or have difficulty in understanding and living. The family and the neighborhood must let it be known that they are aware and united, and that they will not tolerate any form of sexual abuse.

Sr. Thea: Are black family values basically Christian?

Dr. Nichols: They are very Christian. First of all, as Christians and as blacks, we are not judgmental of others. As long as you keep your life style and your pattern of behavior confined to your home or to those with whom you relate, the traditional black community is tolerant and accepting. We don't, for example, talk about illegitimate children in the black community. We talk about the fact that a girl made a mistake, and the community rallies around her, accepts the little baby, and helps her to mature and care for the child, and, if it's at all possible, to continue or further her education. I think that's validated if we look into black communities where blacks have had the responsibility for the schools. We see special programs set up for young women to return to school after they have had their babies. Whereas, in predominantly white communities an unwed mother causes so much scandal that she is out. I think that one of the major focuses of our Christianity as blacks is that we love our neighbors and ourselves. I think perhaps that is the most important facet of black Christianity and specifically black Catholic Christianity.

CHD/Barbara Baker Stephenson

Black Lay Leadership

LAURENCE J. PAYNE, M.A.

WHAT ARE THE PROBLEMS?

What does the Black Catholic Church and its Black leadership in the Black community have to say to the pressures of the Black family?

In most of our parishes from city to city, we still find old Black men and women holding the mantle of leadership, but we find young people who have turned off and dropped out, or who do not have time to devote to the Church because they have to pay for a nice car and other material things which necessitate two jobs. Or we find Blacks in parishes who identify themselves as Blacks only when it is comfortable and convenient.

Do we realize that in every city the plans, the blueprints for where the shopping centers, office buildings, hotels, schools will be built are drawn up ten, fifteen, or twenty years in advance? The land is being bought and sold at this very minute.

As Black Catholics in the Church, where is our plan? Have we done our homework?

What would happen if the Church said to us tomorrow, here is $50 million for the development of the apostolate of the Church in the Black community? Do we have a plan drawn up?

The history of the Church, as with society, in its dealings with Black Americans has been one of displacement. Understanding is needed today by the Church and by society that when you displace me you do it at a cost. The structural interdependence of the relationship must begin to be fully understood.

WHAT OF THE FUTURE?

The majority of Blacks today maintain that if Christianity is to survive in the Black community, it must align itself with the oppressed and concern itself more with the correction of present injustices than with other worldly matters.

The question then becomes not how to bring the 30 million-plus Blacks in America with an average age of twenty-five into the Church; but how to make the Church a more witnessing Church so that those in the Church will remain and others will be attracted to it.

What will become of the three primary social institutions in the Black community—the family, politics, and religion? Each of these institutions generally parallels its counterpart in the larger society, but each has its distinct elements. The differences result from a long history of oppression. There is some evidence that urbanization and improvements in standard of living are minimizing the differences, especially in family patterns and religious practices. The likelihood is, however, that because of the racist nature of American society, and because of increasing Black consciousness, the distinctive aspects of the institutions will persist.

TOWARD THE NEW MILLENNIUM

We stand today on the edge of some of the most cataclysmic social change in the history of our society. We are part of a worldwide social revolution. The electronics revolution has brought great economic problems (a curse and a blessing). We are greatly moved by the drama of our young people (in the schools, colleges, and seminaries) as they struggle and search for new values. Our young are caught up in a seething caldron of social discontent. They are the natural leaders of this new revolution, whether it be concerned with race, class, caste, the environment, sex, politics, economics, or academics.

The old ways of our past are dying before our eyes. Here we stand in the midst of the death of an old order—too often, unprepared to make way for the innovation of the twenty-first century rushing upon us. When we say that conscientious Blacks have died to the American society as it was, we mean that

Laurence J. Payne, M.A., is director of Community Affairs for Catholic Charities in the Archdiocese of St. Paul and Minneapolis. His previous positions include vicar of urban affairs, Diocese of Belleville (Illinois) and director of the Office of Black Ministries, Diocese of Galveston-Houston.

for those Blacks the life style of the twenty-first century has already begun, while the debris, the corruption of the dying twentieth century crash all around us.

Black people in America have borne the stigma of slavery and segregation so long, until every community, white and Black, has been warped by this absurd subjugation. White racism, the creator of this condition, has been the high priest of human distortion in our society. Until Dr. Martin Luther King and others mobilized Blacks against this system, Jim Crow and segregation were supported by laws, mores, and folkways. Even though it has been outlawed, the mark of Cain is still in the land. White America has educated Black and white children with a set of monstrous lies, half-truths, and twisted facts about race.

CHD/Lou Niznik

Both Black and white children, as a result, have been stunted in their mental growth and poisoned in their world outlook. The American white child in the North and South is just as distorted in his thinking as the Black child. The white child has been taught to value race more than humanity. Many white Americans are basically ignorant of the cultures of other people, and have no appreciation for any other language, art, religion, history, or ethical system save their own. They are in no way prepared to live in a multiracial, multicultural society without hostility, bigotry, and intolerance. A cursory check of most white educational institutions (their boards, their curriculum, their faculty makeup, their student body makeup, their commitment to inclusion and power, etc.) will find them in 1985, where most of them were in 1953—operating out of the blissful ignorance of either tokenism or benevolent paternalism—both of which are carryovers from the dying past of racism. White American institutions have been conditioned to support a mythology which believes that:

- it must convert all people into "good Americans";
- all scholarly thought arises out of Anglo conformity to Greco-Roman and European world views;
- all must similarly express themselves culturally (dress, think, pray, and amuse ourselves as Europeans);
- every socio-economical-political system must epitomize the values of our mechanistic and materialistic society;
- American values are idealistic and altruistic;
- America is a democratic and Christian nation while all other nations are totalitarian, unchristian, pagan, and primitive.

We as Black Catholic laypersons must develop a powerful set of new values to both counteract the venom of racism and maintain group sanity. We are still faced with centuries of distortion where Black children have been taught to:

- hate and despise themselves—the cause of much conflict and fratricide among our youth;
- imitate people (books, pictures, movies, etc.) who they have been taught to believe are superior;
- believe that Blacks had no history, no culture, nor anything Black of worth or meaning;
- view the world as one-dimensional: white, Western, Greco-Roman in culture, Christian, democratic, and Protestant in ethic;
- believe that the non-Western or oriental world is primitive in culture, heathen in religion, pagan in ethics, communistic in economics, and totalitarian in politics.

But we live in a multiracial, multicultural world in which there are many cultures, religious beliefs, and socio-economic-political systems. Whether we want to or not, our children must receive a multicultural education to live creatively in this new world.

Conducted in a variety of circumstances and directed to widely diverse audiences, catechetical activity takes many forms. There is catechesis for different age levels—children, preadolescents and adolescents, young adults and adults—and for different groups (e.g., the non-English speaking, members of particular cultural, racial and ethnic groups, the handicapped, etc.) within each category. It will also vary in form according to the language, vocation, abilities, and geographical location of those catechized. Its components include sharing faith life, experiencing liturgical worship, taking part in Christian service, and participating in religious instruction.

We need a new social philosophy to achieve this.

A broadened knowledge of all world religions, world cultures, and all racial and nationalistic strains which make up the human family will make this ethic possible.

THE BLACK CATHOLIC CHALLENGE

Black people, since 1619, have been about the task of stirring up the gift of God that is within us. Through these mighty gifts of the Spirit we shall create a new world of Americans. Fortunately for many Black people, all Black people were not blighted by ignorance of our heritage. Some of us have been products of experiences where this healing stream removed society's venom from our pathway. Our stream of consciousness informs us that human personality is potentially divine, hence our destiny must be spiritual. All America is suffering and dying for lack of this new humanism. A new century lends promise that the color line will be ended. We of the Black Catholic world, along with our Black brothers and sisters of all denominations, are gathering in the spiritual strength necessary to build this new and better world for our children. Many of us may die trying to give birth to this new age in the midst of a dying century (as indeed many already have), but our progeny will raise their spirits beyond the dream of a brave new world. They will occupy the citadels of this new world. We are not alone in this vision of a new order; we are not alone in our beauty and strength. We are part of all mankind who throughout all recorded time have bravely fought and nobly died in order to be free. It is upon this foundation that we now stand, that we now build our Church.

"Black Lay Leadership," Laurence J. Payne, copyright © 1980 *The City of God: A Journal of Urban Ministry*, Vol. 2 No. 1 (Summer 1980), St. Maur Hospitality Center, V. Rev. Ivan W. Hughes, OSB, editor. Reprinted with permission.

Since historically the Black Church and the Black family continue to be the most viable institutions in the Black community, it is necessary for Black church people, to confront effectively those community issues and other institutions that are capable of either destroying or nurturing Black family life.

Andrew Billingsley, Ph.D.
Black Families and the Struggle for Survival

CHD/Peter Magubane

Black and Catholic

Fr. Edward K. Braxton, Ph.D., S.T.D.

Black Catholics in America are, paradoxically, the enviable bearers of several traditions. Many have a deep commitment to the Catholic tradition and the American democratic experiment. Both of these are Western European in origin. A large number are converts from Protestant (particularly Baptist) traditions that link them to a strong reformation heritage. All share a tortured but proud history: the civil rights movement, relentless segregation and oppression before, during, and after the enactment of Jim Crow laws, the emancipation, the Civil War, the years of enslavement and fragmented memories and visions of what life may have been in the motherland. Heroes and heroines of family, Church, the arts, sports, social, political, and intellectual life shine like stars through those years.

James Cone judges many of the speculative questions of white, Western theology to be without meaning for blacks since they were not asked in the context of the black experience. But what constitutes the black experience? What individuals or groups constitute the "accrediting agency" that authenticates one's vocabulary, opinions, attitudes, social and intellectual concerns, artistic and cultural preferences, and personal life styles as being genuinely *black*? It is an empirical fact that in the United States many different experiences contribute to the complex, multifaceted reality of black life.

Many blacks are joining the Muslim religion, while others follow no religion at all. Neither the "Missa Luba" nor Negro spirituals are meaningful to some. Black Americans may be politically to the right, to the left, or, as in other groups, politically indifferent. While educational and employment opportunities are far from ideal, more and more black people receive technical training, advanced degrees, and positions of influence. While the number of black people who are poor and unemployed in urban centers remains high, the suburbs and even farm life are not foreign to the black experience. More subtly, while the media and the times have settled upon the designation *black*, all do not embrace it. Many prefer designations such as Negro, African, Afro-American, American, or simply people of color. Still others think of themselves only as human beings. Race, for them, is a secondary reality that merits neither discrimination nor special treatment.

Alex Haley's *Roots* has been much applauded for making an urgent case for the reappropriation of the African roots of the American black community, but it need not follow that all subsequent historical, social, and cultural influences must be rejected. In a general way, the black experience may be found in a common color, culture, and consciousness. But if these are given too narrow an interpretation, certain modes of thought, styles of prayer, idioms of discourse, and social and political priorities will effectively become normative in the black community. Blacks have rejected white stereotypes. They must not yield to stereotypes of their own making. This would clearly constrain the self-expression of a community that is obviously quite diverse.

In the end, it appears difficult and perhaps undesirable to define the black experience. This may be equally true of the black religious experience and the black Catholic experience. But definition is not the only way to give expression to a reality. As diverse expressions develop and mature, black Catholics may be in a position to enrich theological literature and religious life in America with classic expressions of their unique history.

It is evident that great classics in both our secular and religious traditions are at once deeply personal and particular in their origins and mode of expression, but public and universal in their power to transform the human spirit—works that speak to the hearts and minds even of those who know nothing of that particular heritage. Louis Armstrong and Billie Holliday created very special musical forms in American jazz and blues. Yet their works are universally acclaimed as classics, because they have the singular capacity to enrich and move any attentive person who hears the music.

Fr. Edward K. Braxton, Ph.D., S.T.D., holds his Ph.D. in religious studies and S.T.D. in systematic theology from the Pontifical Faculty of the Catholic University of Louvain in Belgium. His writings have appeared in the *Harvard Theological Review, Theological Studies, Chicago Studies, Commonweal, America,* and other journals. His book, *The Wisdom Community,* was published in 1980. A priest of the Archdiocese of Chicago, Fr. Braxton is director of Calvert House, the Catholic Student Center at the University of Chicago.

In our culture, we have a great need for new expressions of classic power. More and more, the period piece eclipses the classic in popular culture. Consider Benchley's *Jaws* favored over Melville's *Moby Dick* or Segal's *Love Story* favored over Shakespeare's *Romeo and Juliet*. Due to its intrinsic force, one need not personally have the experiences portrayed by the classic in order to be touched, confronted, and renewed by the penetrating understanding of life that it discloses. One need not be a member of a problem-laden Irish-American family in order to be stunned and challenged by an experience of Eugene O'Neill's *Long Day's Journey Into Night.* Nor need one have personal experience of the special pains and tragedies of black urban tenement dwellers in order to participate in the catharsis of Lorraine Hansberry's classic play, *A Raisin in the Sun*. All that is needed is sensitivity that recognizes oneself in the story of Everyman.

Sr. Angela Williams

One hopes that the Catholic Church will continue to develop a sense of unity in diversity. Such an openness to liturgical, theological, doctrinal, and juridical pluralism would make it possible for the Church to be enhanced by the gifts of black religious men and women. Pope Paul VI has rightly declared that the Catholic Church very much needs these gifts at this moment in history. If this patrimony is nurtured, it might focus the Church anew on the meaning and purpose of the Christian religion with telling and classic urgency.

What are the fundamental or foundational social and political concerns and goals of black Catholics? How are these related to the theological foundations and social teachings of the Catholic tradition: Are they complementary or contradictory? Are certain Catholic "doctrines" functionally irrelevant for many black Catholics? Which ones? Why? Do the experiences of black Catholic families provide new understanding and raise new questions regarding moral questions that touch marriage and family life?

It is time to explore the points of contact between the black Catholic experience and black theology in a systematic way. How can the underlying realities of the generic Christian faith of foundations, the specific Catholic beliefs of doctrines and theoretical constructs of systematics be theologically, liturgically, and pastorally enriched by the experience of black Catholicism? Can the visions of black theology as it has developed in the black Protestant community be simply transported into the Catholic community? Are there elements in black theology that are incompatible with traditional Catholic theology? Is this due to a flaw at the foundation or to different cultural contexts? Can current developments in Catholic theology help to meet some of the criticisms that are being raised concerning black theology? Can black theology help the Catholic Church to understand new aspects of its Catholicity? How can the Church best communicate its deepest and most authentic religious genius in a way that nurtures the dignity and self-esteem of every member of the black community and hence builds up the Body of Christ? What concrete efforts and commitment of resources are being directed to adult religious education in the black community? As important as Catholic schools may be in the black community, the adult members of the community will never be fully at home in the Church if they are not encouraged to develop a mature and adult understanding of the Christian faith.

The 1980s will be a crucial time for the Catholic Church and the black community in America. It can be a time of growing credibility and mutual enhancement. If the Catholic Church follows the discouraging pattern of the larger white society, which appears to be content with token advances while closing its eyes to policies and programs that perpetuate domestic injustice, a fitting time, or *kairos*, may be lost.

"Black and Catholic," Rev. Edward K. Braxton, originally published in AMERICA, Vol. 142 No. 12 (March 29, 1980). Reprinted with permission of the author.

Black and Catholic

Sr. FRANCESCA THOMPSON, OSF, Ph.D.

The Catholic Church claims we are God's Church: God-originated and God-sustained. We are emissaries of the King, ambassadors for the kingdom. How dare we trumpet thus and not live up to that which the King has advocated: "I came that all men might have life and have it more abundantly"? He never said he came for some. He never proclaimed that the Good News was for the privileged rich. Whether there are whites who erroneously believe it or not, there was no back door in the stable of Bethlehem for the black king to enter and adore God, though Scripture tells us that it is the poor, the downtrodden, the neglected by and shunned of society that must be our first concern.

Where has the Church stood on the issue of race and racial discrimination? Where does it stand today? Where do our bishops stand? Oh, yes! I dare question and question because I love the Church. I want it to become at long last what God has intended that it become, a home for all his children, regardless of race or nationality. I want it to be in the vanguard in regard to justice. I do believe that the Holy Spirit, who breathes justice, calls us to lead the army of those who fight against all injustice, wherever and whenever it appears. I want my Church not only to have its doors open to my people, I want its arms extended to bid them come and be filled with life-giving streams when they get there. The Church may reply: "We have always been on the side of the oppressed. Witness our very presence in oppressed areas." It is not enough! I, as one who stood there in the midst of the oppressed, know it is not enough to stand in the presence of the oppressed. We must stand with and beside those who labor, fight, and die (if need be) that justice may triumph in our justice-starved world.

My Church must evidence a hierarchy richly interspersed with black bishops. My Church must promote and encourage black vocations so that our black youth can see models of right and righteousness among their very own. My Church must make itself comfortable and familiar to my black brothers and sisters who have grown out of a different climate when it comes to theology and religious perspectives. I want my Church to become as real, as vital, and as alive as any other Church is to black people. I want my Church to be a Church where my brothers and sisters can find the God who created them and find his words ringing true. "Come to me all you who labor and are heavily burdened and I will give you rest." I want our spirituals, which have grown out of the black experience in this country, to be sung in our churches so that black people can hear and know that the Church is not separated from the struggle that faces them each and every day of their living. I want black people to learn and see it evidenced that we are all together in this struggle for freedom from oppression. Those who do not struggle against it are on the side of those who perpetrate it.

CHD/Michal Heron

My Church must be, with God, on the side of those who sing and, deep in their hearts, strain to believe. "We ain't in no ways tired . . . come so far from where we been. Nobody said the road would be easy, but I don't believe he'd bring me this far to leave me." My Church must not leave the strugglers. The Church must join them—hand in hand, heart to heart—so that together we may overcome the injustice that apparently runs rampant and reigns supreme in our world today.

What I am saying, I suppose, is that I don't want my Church to simply mouth rhetoric about injustice. I don't want my Church merely to preach and rail against it. I want my Church in the forefront—seen, heard, and its great influence felt—with those who actively engage in combat, those who fight vigorously—God-inspired and God-strengthened—against any and all injustice. I hope that it is not too much for a very proud and yet ever-devoted, loving, black daughter to ask or to expect from her Holy Mother Church.

Sr. Francesca Thompson, OSF, Ph.D., who is assistant to the dean of Fordham University in New York City, holds a doctorate in speech and theater from the University of Michigan. She lectures frequently throughout the country on a variety of topics including Black literary artists, Black poetry, Black drama, and justice and interracial questions.

"Black and Catholic," Francesca Thompson, OSF, originally published in AMERICA, Vol. 142 No. 12 (March 29, 1980). Reprinted with permission of the author.

The Black Family An Intimate Language

Sr. EVA MARIE LUMAS, SSS, M.A.

Religious educators in Black parishes frequently ask in bewilderment, and sometimes in anger, "What do Black parents want from the Church?"

Catholic parents want the Church to help them parent their children. Black Catholic parents want the Church to help them parent their children—their Black children. Catholic parents want their parishes to actualize their potential as *extended family* by facilitating programs to meet the actual needs of its people. In the context of Black parishes, extended family are those people who share the hopes, know the hardships, esteem the heritage, affirm the strengths, and address the existential realities of Black people. For Blacks, that's family. That is what Black Catholic parents want from the Church!

The Black family has traditionally constituted a counterstance for Blacks to the influences of a hostile society. Black parents have had to teach their children to interact within a society that devaluates them without personal destruction, embitterment, or despair. Family life is essential to the survival of Black people. Successful parenting *and* extended family are crucial to the effectiveness of family life. Black parents need to be capable, responsible, and resourceful adults in order to successfully parent. Hurting children are the progeny of hurting adults—adults whose hopes, abilities, supports, information, and experience have not prepared them to deal meaningfully with the existential realities of their lives. Black parents need the parish to listen to them, to collaborate with them, and to avail its resources to them. That is what Black Catholic parents want from the Church!

Parent programs must give Blacks an experience of their own worth and competence. Only then can they positively participate in the development of their children. The Church must invest itself in the nurturing of Black adults because it is ultimately their responsibility to teach Black children to interpret their lived-experience, to envision their future, and to cherish their heritage. Black parents who are confident that life is a gift, regardless of the headaches and heartbreaks, will ensure the positive development of Black children. These parents will help to design and implement programs for Black children and youths, as well as to become a support for other Black adults.

Content possibilities for parent programs are infinite. They extend from faith development to recreation, from effective budgeting to leadership skills, from enhancing interpersonal relationships to participating in neighborhood self-improvement groups. Anything that affects the lives of Black parents is appropriate content for parent programs in Black communities. Anything that is values-laden, as all things are, is an appropriate area for the Church to be engaged in.

"What do Black Catholic parents want from the Church?" They want *extended family*. They want a faith community that is intrinsically bound up in the dialogue of the intimate language that is *family*. They want a fellowship with a people who touches their lives with an obvious investment in their well-being.

Just as parents need support to successfully parent, parent programs need the support of all the other ministries of the parish. The intent of programs must be clear. The way in which varied parish ministries relate to the overall mission of the parish must be clear, deliberate, and intentional. If a parish program is designed in a vacuum, participants will soon discover that the program director has written a check that the local faith community can't cash!

Black Catholic parents are not asking the Church to do something new. They are asking the Church to *actualize its potential as extended family* in a new way, in a way that resonates with the requirements of our age and the consciousness of today's Black people.

Sr. Eva Marie Lumas, SSS, M.A., is the Christian education consultant for Black communities for the Diocese of Oakland (California). She is also Christian-education program coordinator and publications editor for the National Black Sisters' Conference. Sr. Eva Marie lectures widely and writes on Christian education from a Black perspective.

Black parents need programs that have

a. Leaders who know and esteem Black people
b. Leaders who know and identify with the Black pilgrimage in America
c. Methods that employ sound adult-education principles
d. Methods that reflect an understanding of how Black people deliberate, articulate, and celebrate their reality
e. Content that addresses the lived reality of Blacks

Parish ministers should enter into dialogue with their people while steeping themselves in sound literature.

Our Church is missioned to affirm and to challenge, to learn and to teach, to mourn tragedy and to celebrate triumphs, to receive and to give life. Our Church must facilitate opportunities for Black parents to identify, preserve, and implement positive values and effective skills, so that Black families can continue to combat the effects of racism in America. In that way, the Church will be extended family to Black parents, to Black families. Only when the Catholic Church has extended its vision and resources to Blacks in such a way that Black people themselves can attest to the Catholic Church's investment in them, will the Church be extended family to Black families. When the Catholic Church participates in the activity and shares the responsibility of successful parenting in Black communities, it will speak the intimate language of the family to Black parents. That is what Black Catholic parents want from the Church!

"The Black Family: An Intimate Language," Sr. Eva Marie Lumas, SSS, Paper presented to Hope for Families Conference, Houston (1980). Reprinted with permission of the author.

CHD/Barbara Baker Stephenson

The Black Family that Is Church

TOINETTE M. EUGENE, PH.D.

The promotion of family life is clearly one of the central concerns of the Roman Catholic Church in the decade of the eighties.[1] The 1980 Synod of Bishops in Rome was devoted specifically to a study of this topic. Pope John Paul II published his Apostolic Exhortation, *Familiaris Consortio*, as a resumé and response which strongly recommended that bishops' conferences study the elements of their cultures regarding marriage and family "to achieve authentic inculturation in theological, pastoral, liturgical, and disciplinary areas."[2] Moreover, American Catholic bishops have repeatedly expressed their concern over the disintegration of the family in the United States.

If, indeed, this priority is clearly a primary one for the Church in this decade, then we cannot escape the logical need to address this concern for family life from the black Catholic perspective. It is obvious that real insight into the factors that build up or tear down *The family that is Church* can be achieved only by serious study of the culture, the society, and political-economic factors. Such a study must also encompass religious structures, and theological belief systems that surround and support black families. To explore aspects of black family life within the context of the Catholic Church, consideration will be given in this essay to three areas: (1) sociological perspectives on the black family; (2) black love and black family spirituality and (3) evangelization and catechesis for the black community as extended family.

Rogelio Solis/Courtesy of Mississippi Today

THE FAMILY THAT IS CHURCH: GENERAL REFLECTIONS

Every summer, we solemnly celebrate Pentecost with the pomp and splendor that the "Birthday of the Church" deserves. In the very miracle and message of the Pentecost event, we discover that God chose to be spoken of and revealed to men and women in their *own* language and culture. In the Pentecost event, the gift of God's Spirit was proclaimed in a context of cultural pluralism in order that all those gathered could experience fully the richness of God alive in their midst.

The story of Pentecost and the evangelizing action of God as revealed in Acts 2:1-47 offer a theological and pastoral methodology that ought not be refused. The point the Scripture makes is that the Word of God must be contextualized (i.e., inculturated) for any people to become "Church", and in order that the Good News may be understood and accepted completely as it was intended. Our religious experiences and theological expressions must be paralleled and permeated by cultural and sociological experience that is indigenous and familiar to the particular grouping. Only in that way can the community, the family, and each individual belonging to it, become and remain believers without violation of either spiritual or ethnic integrity.

SOCIOLOGICAL PERSPECTIVES ON THE BLACK FAMILY

One of the intriguing sociological developments of the last twenty years has been heightened interest in black family systems and life styles. Far more than the general study of the family in modern society, interest in black families has been much more controversial and intensive. In part, this ongoing investigative interest is a consequence of the unique history of black people in the United States as a racial minority oppressed by economic and racial barriers. It is also a consequence of their continued quest for survival.[3]

It seems important to review some sociological perspectives because the social scientific investigation, study, and description of black families, upon which pastoral knowledge and practice might be based, have been characterized by myths, stereotypes, and invalidated generalizations. Further, it is important to point out that most social science research on black families has not been studies of marriage and family among blacks. Instead, the focus has been

Toinette M. Eugene, Ph.D., serves as assistant professor of education, society, and Black church studies at Colgate Rochester Divinity School in Rochester, New York. Dr. Eugene has published a variety of articles and essays concerning Black Catholicism and religious education.

on race relations, aggression, the so-called Negro problem, poverty, and the like.[4]

A review of sociological literature from the 1920s to the 1960s provides a striking parallel between the study of black families and three sociological fields: social problems, social disorganization, and social pathology. It was within the context of this pathological framework that black families were investigated, and negatively compared with the so-called nuclear white family. However, the assumption that the isolated nuclear family is the only family form which can best serve the needs of a modern industrial society has been seriously challenged, on the grounds that a pluralistic society requires differential family structures in order to meet fully the needs of its members as well as those of the social system.

Even given the current media concern over single-parent families raising their children, of gay couples being given custody of their children, the failure to recognize the viability of varied black family structures has frequently resulted in a comparison with some presumed ideal white norm that portrayed black families as pathological, weak, bad, or inferior. Just as the "blackness" concept has been portrayed through the ages in literature, religion, history, folklore, and social customs as evil, and as an abyss of hopelessness and eternal damnation, American black *families* have meant a "tangle of pathology."[5] The Moynihan Report served as an inaccurate and racist summary condemnation, describing matriarchy, child illegitimacy, adultery, divorce, desertion, welfare dependency, low school achievement, low educational aspirations, juvenile delinquency, and adult crime as inherent characteristics of the black family.

This description is now under heavy attack by black and white sociologists. For we are now in a period in which research on black families can be characterized as "beyond pathology." Andrew Billingsley helped to lead the way with the publication of *Black Families in White America* in 1968, followed in 1970 by Charles V. Willie's edited volume, *The Family Life of Black People. The Black Family: Essays and Studies* by Robert Staples, and John Scanzoni's *The Black Family in Modern Society* were published in 1971, followed by Robert B. Hill's monograph, *The Strengths of Black Families* in 1972. This seminal literature has resulted in the development of new conceptualizations, theoretical perspectives, and an increasing understanding of the dynamics of black family life which have bearing on our positive pastoral knowledge, practice, and efforts at building a parish community based on the black family that is Church. This new body of growing literature on black families overwhelmingly suggests systemic changes and systemic blame rather than individual change and victim blame.

More recent literature on black families has begun to identify and emphasize those factors which support the development of stable families. Billingsley refers to these factors as "opportunity screens" and suggests that they have enabled some black families to survive and to move beyond survival to stability and social achievement.[6] These opportunity screens include

CHD/Peter Magubane

1. A set of values or philosophy with an accompanying pattern of behavior consistent with those values, and a certain degree of independence and control of the forces affecting the lives of their members
A corollary to this is that the broader black Church has always functioned in this way as a value giver and value guardian for the black community. It could well afford to do so, since the leadership is black and its ordained pastors also have family obligations as spouses and parents. In this historical tradition, the black family that is also the black Church understands itself as *self-ministering* (that is, had sufficient numbers of ordained black leadership); *self-sustaining* (that is, financially independent or interdependent; in other words, not considered primarily a mission); *and self-propagating* (that is, fully responsible for its own increase in numbers and for the educational advancement of its members).

The implications of this first opportunity screen, and its corollary, are pregnant with challenge and potential for black Catholic parishes. The implications are significant with regard to black ordained leadership, respected black lay leadership, finances, evangelization, worship, catechesis, and pastoral planning for the future. The issue must be raised and concrete projections must be made at diocesan and parish levels regarding the development of black Catholic lay and ordained ministers, for financial responsibility based on an equitable system of interdependence, and for black participation in the decision-making processes of the diocese and the parish.

2. Strong religious convictions and behavior

An implication of this is that there is an operative religious educational system which does transmit via the family that is Church, Catholic doctrine, tradition, images of God, and appropriate actions which follow upon being religious persons who belong to a believing community. Religious convictions and behavior must be supported by family participation in pastoral opportunities, which grow out of the needs expressed in the home. Family rituals, prayers, celebrations, and even confrontations in the black community need the educational input of Scripture, liturgical nurture and reconciliation, and pastoral care which the larger Church must offer.

3. Education or educational aspirations of one or more members

An implication for this in Catholic tradition weighs heavily on how much we value, support, subsidize, and provide Catholic education through Catholic schools in the black community as a way of sustaining and enriching the black family structure. The history of Catholic schools closing because of the lack of parish, diocesan, or religious congregations' support is worth mentioning here as a value indicator of how the institutional Catholic Church communicates with the black community on a socioeconomic basis.

Catholic schools and Catholic education have long been the source for *converts* and for religious and priestly *vocations* within the black community. Predictably, the absence of Catholic schools or their dwindling presence hurts everyone if there is no creative replacement for this component of a local parish unit. Beyond the concern for parochial school education, there is also responsibility on the part of parishes serving black families for expanding the quality of teaching and learning in the public school system. The values of the family as a sacred institution, the significance of human dignity, and the fostering of personal pride in self must be addressed and encouraged through black and Catholic pastoral presence within the public education system.

4. Economic security

For Billingsley, this opportunity screen means possession of property, or ownership of that which is lasting and permanent. An implication of this for the black family that is Church entails status as a respected parish on an equal footing (i.e., not a "mission" church) with other local churches in a diocese, and thus not dependent on handouts based on diocesan or wealthy parishes' good will. It entails provision for the economic security and advancement of family members through such means as parish, deanery, or diocesan-sponsored or supported conferences on employment opportunities, and community organizing. For the family, security is tied to having a place or a home of one's own. The pastoral implications of sponsoring or supporting low-income housing for families or senior citizens are clear. Advocacy with regard to tenants' rights, the possibility of developing parish cooperatives for day care so that mothers may seek employment are related to furthering this economic security opportunity screen.

The final two opportunity screens of Billingsley may be briefly listed here:

5. Family ties

6. Community centered activities

Similarly, Robert Hill has identified five black family strengths in his convincing and cogent monograph aptly titled, *The Strengths of Black Families.* They are

a. strong kinship bonds
b. strong work orientation
c. adaptability of family roles

d. strong achievement orientation
e. strong religious orientation

In another investigation, John Scanzoni in *The Black Family in Modern Society* identified a similar list of opportunity factors for black families. These include

a. economic status advantage over the black population nationally
b. residence in and length of exposure to urban milieu
c. strong family ties
d. support and aid from community figures and role models
e. religious affiliation and involvement
f. positive school experiences
g. positive self-image

A cursory cross-referencing of these studies indicates that which is clearly common to sustain black families: religious convictions, affiliation, and involvement are critical; religious and secular education are of primary importance; kinship ties, family bonds, and marital relationships come to our attention.

What seems appropriate and useful is to take the key issues raised in these studies—issues that speak of supporting the stability in the black family—and use them to enrich pastoral ministry and an understanding of the black community as an extended system.

USCC/Lou Niznik

BLACK LOVE AND BLACK FAMILY SPIRITUALITY

One way of describing and defining family spirituality is to realize that each family is a little church. The family is, so to speak, "the domestic Church, a community of faith living in hope and love, serving God, and the entire human family,"[7] the World Synod of Bishops says. Everyone's first parish is experienced in his or her own family. Each of us encounters Jesus and God first in the Christian community, which is made up of our parents and our extended immediate family. Innumerable children wonder sometime early in the game, "Is Daddy God?" Or perhaps it is a grandmother or an impressive uncle who is the object of the question.

Whether expressed or not, our initial notions of God are very often translations from the experience of our own parents. We say, "God is our Father," although we try not to say it with too many sexist overtones. What we understand by "God" is colored by what we understand of father or parent in our own lives. We say, "God is love." What love is or can be is first of all a projection of the love we have experienced in our own family life. Of course, it works the other way too, and our mature understanding of fatherhood or parenthood and love is also shaped by the revelation of how God is and of how God "does" us! Nevertheless, as children, our encounter with God, and with all transcendent values, is colored by our family life. Later, that coloring will be modified but never entirely blotted out.

How people feel about the Church too, is in large measure, determined by how they feel about the first community that they experienced—their family. If that was essentially a good experience, they will eventually be able to trust the wider community of parish church, at least when it acts more as family than as a bureaucratic institution which is coldly impersonal. All this is true of families in general, but it is also true of black families in particular, since the black family also plays a central role in the socialization and Christianization of its members.[8]

The notion that God is love is a central issue for developing an authentic black family spirituality. Black love must be understood as a moral, ethical, and divine imperative for formulating a theologically based catechesis for the black community.[9]

Without a doubt, the agency for gospel liberation and the strongest asset of the black community is "black love." It is the chief attribute of the black family, and that which predicates pride of ancestry and willingness to include prodigal children, outcasts, the pariah, the stranger, and even the oppressor within the folds of its embrace. Historically, black love has enabled the momentarily crushed spirits of black folk to look beyond the immediacy of present suffering to a God who has never forsaken them in the hour of anguish and despair. It has been the religious aspect of black love that has prompted black Christians always to consider the worth of all human life: born and unborn; legitimate and "illegitimate"; single or several times married; old, unemployed, young, and inexperienced—all in terms of the accomplishment of God's will expressed in the here and now. "Love one another as I have loved you" is an invitation that the black family has accepted and acted upon in ways that may be clearly differentiated from those of white families who are also Church.

In many instances, black love has driven away the bitterness and hatred which would predispose black people to denounce the entire Christian tradition as inveterately racist, not to mention sexist and imperialistic. But behind black Christian love is the Christ who teaches that bitterness must be dispelled with *effective* compassion and *affective* justice toward the oppressors who also need liberation through the redemptive power of God.

Martin Luther King, Jr., has demonstrated overwhelmingly with the witness of his life that black Christian love forms good moral character, good religious leadership, and good prophetic judgment. He has also convinced the black Christian community of the applicability of the love of God as a central ingredient for a Christian social ethic which must bear prophetic incisiveness. The black family must articulate a spirituality which can inspire parents, children, and other relatives in their extended grouping to attain that caliber of self-sacrificial love and concern for others. Similarly, a black family spirituality needs to persuade the black community that is Church that it too stands ultimately under the judgment of God.

The black family is Church. To be Church, it must model what the Church is in a more intimate sense: it must be the Sacrament of God and Christ, as the Church in general is. The black family must be the place where the mystery of God's love for humanity is celebrated in word and action, in prayer, and in ritual. The spirituality of the black family is not a spirituality for the family alone, but it must articulate and announce to society and to the world in which it lives the Kingdom of God and the Good News of Jesus the Liberator.

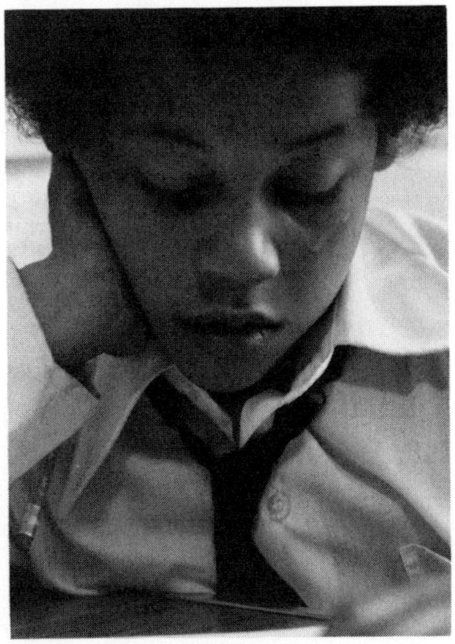
USCC/Nelson Brooks

EVANGELIZATION AND CATECHESIS THAT SUSTAINS THE BLACK FAMILY

It seems obvious that a truly black articulation, which is evangelizing and educative for and by black Catholic families, is crucial to the religious survival of that Church community. It is also essential for the mature faith development of the larger Catholic community. Black articulation becomes fluent in presenting Catholic catechesis through its use of interpretation and indigenization as effective means of transmitting the Word of God. The articulation of black life experienced in a variety of ways in light of Christian faith makes for holistic and homey catechesis.

In offering some limited examples to illustrate areas of need and in raising the question of what must be developed at further stages, it is important to state concisely some essentials and sources for an effective black catechesis.[10]

1. There is a need within evangelization, pastoral renewal programs, and religious education programs for stressing the importance of the black religious experience.

In this context, it is implicitly understood that "black experience" is not monolithic. Black experience is a source for training religious leaders and catechists because it seeks, when properly and fully developed, to relate the situation of black people in America to the biblical Word and ongoing revelation of God. This means that black Catholic catechesis cannot speak of God and divine activity without identifying this with the liberation of the black community and all oppressed communities. We need to tell not only of the universal goodness of the Lord, but of God's particular goodness to them right here in the home, the neighborhood, the parish where they live.

2. The knowledge of black history, religious and secular, is essential for those who lead and teach in the black Catholic community.

Being able to tell the Black Story is necessary because it clearly displays the determination of a people who would be liberated from all oppression. To tell the Black Story is essential because it is a ritual recounting of the traditions; a ceremonial recapturing of the values, the wisdom, and the spirit of a people which is able to overcome enslavement and to press forward into a freeing future despite life's many contradictions and hardships. The story of our black foreparents, becomes at once a martyrology, a litany of the saints, a model for imitation in life, and a praxis for further liberation.

3. The development of black culture is an essential element to be expressed within the context of a black catechesis.

Culture, which shapes the ethos of a people, simultaneously forms and reflects its values. It also determines a people's notions about the purpose of life, the relationship between the physical and spiritual, and the role of the transcendent in life. Culture is the natural foundation on which religion must be built. Consequently, successful evangelization and catechesis within the black community can only begin with a basic reverence, respect, and knowledge of that culture which resides within it.

4. Revelation needs to be stressed as an essential source for a black articulation in catechesis.

Revelation means, of course, what God is doing every day in human history on behalf of oppressed people, and in their own personal history. Scripture is the quintessential aspect of revelation, revealing Jesus Christ and his Resurrection event, which is the clue and key to what catechesis is all about, working within the black experience. The Resurrection event does not, however, downplay the suffering and a theology of the cross from which black people draw courage, resiliency, and a sense of solidarity with a wounded Savior.

5. Working in a church structure bound by tradition, the use of tradition as a freeing element for a black Catholic catechesis must be creative.

A black articulation must of necessity focus as much on the broader Christian tradition of the black Church in America as it does on that of white, Western Catholicism. The faith that has sustained black Catholic families is a faith rooted firmly in their past. Now it needs to be articulated more strongly still, with a bold consciousness of needs and aspirations as a black community in the present and in the future. The heritage of black Catholics cannot be separated from the historic relationship with the broader dimensions of the black Church without danger of seriously distorting the connections among all black people in this country who are in a significant sense, "extended family."[11]

CONCLUSIONS

This essay has endeavored to highlight a recognition of the black family as an expression of the ecclesial mystery which became a reality through the Gift of God's Spirit at Pentecost. The black family that is Church possesses a distinct history, a value system, patterns of behavior, truths and persons which it holds dear, and which can be described, understood, and appreciated for their own beauty, strengths, and characteristics.

Real concern for the promotion of black family life and ministry involves a wide-eyed familiarity with the human context of the men, women, and children who would form the family that is Church. One of the principal legacies of Vatican II and the 1980 Synod of Bishops is its insistence on dialogue with the world and especially with the social sciences, which help to build up the process of sustaining healthy human relationships. The ongoing task of Pentecost as it is lived out, particularly in the lives of the Black Catholic community and its ministers, is to understand more fully and to act more committedly on the belief that *we are family*. Since black Catholic families are, in this sense, the source of the Church's life and growth in the broader black community, the measure of ministry to black families will determine the quality of mission in the world.

CHD/Lou Niznik

NOTES

1. See Clarissa W. Atkinson, "American Families and 'The American Family': Myths and Realities," *Harvard Divinity Bulletin* (December 1981–January 1982): 10–13; Bishop J. Francis Stafford, "The Year of the Family Revisited," *America* 144 (May 16, 1981): 399–403.

2. "The Message to Christian Families in the Modern World," the 1980 World Synod of Bishops' Statement in *Origins* 10 (November 6, 1980): 326. In a commentary, the editor notes that in the course of the synod deliberations on the family, numerous addresses were given on inculturation and adaptation of church practice to differing cultural situations.

3. See Andrew Billingsley, *Black Families and the Struggle for Survival* (New York: Friendship Press, 1974); Herbert G. Gutman, *The Black Family in Slavery and Freedom, 1750–1925* (New York: Pantheon Books, 1976).

4. Doris Y. Wilkinson, "Toward a Positive Frame of Reference for Analysis of Black Families," *Journal of Marriage and the Family* 40 (November 1978): 707–8.

5. See Lee Rainwater and William L. Yancey, eds., *The Moynihan Report and the Politics of Controversy: A Trans-action Social Science and Public Policy Report* (Cambridge: MIT Press, 1967). (This book includes the full text of *The Negro Family: The Case for National Action* by Daniel Patrick Moynihan.)

6. Andrew Billingsley, "Screens of Opportunity," in *Black Families in White America* (Englewood Cliffs, N.J.: Prentice-Hall), 97–104.

7. "The Message to Christian Families," 324. The Synod of Bishops appears to be reiterating the more basic tenet on the family as the first cell of the Church as set forth in the *Dogmatic Constitution of the Church*, no. 11, in *The Documents of Vatican II* (New York: America Press, 1966), 29.

8. For an excellent theological treatment of the unique relationship between the two institutions of the black family and the Church, see J. Deotis Roberts, *Roots of a Black Future: Family and Church* (Philadelphia: Westminster Press, 1980).

9. Calvin E. Bruce, "Refocusing Black Religious Education: Three Imperatives," *Religious Education* 69 (July–August 1974): 421–32.

10. For a more precise and detailed rendering of these sections on "Love and Spirituality" and on "Evangelization and Catechesis," see Toinette M. Eugene, "Developing Black Catholic Belief: Catechesis as a Black Articulation of the Faith," in *Theology: A Portrait in Black* (Pittsburgh: Capuchin Press, 1980), 140–60.

11. For a more technical explanation of the concept of "extended family," which is useful for pastoral applications regarding how extended families are formed and how they function, see Elmer P. Martin and Joanne Mitchell Martin, *The Black Extended Family* (Chicago: University of Chicago Press, 1978).

Courtesy of Marian College

PART III

Our Response

We become
FAMILY
COMMUNITY
CHURCH
by sharing
LIFE.

In
Family
Community
Church
We grow to
FULLNESS
of
LIFE.

Circle of Family, Community, Church

Sr. Thea Bowman, FSPA, Ph.D.

Look at the inner circle of the diagram. Everybody needs family. We start with the basic human need for family and for one another. We realize that one father, one mother are not enough; that families need the support of other families, and so we seek ways of bonding, nourishing, and healing.

Look now at the wider circle. We become community when families share values and needs. This bonding strengthens and nourishes us. The love that makes us community also makes us truly Church.

Look at the outside circle. The Church formalizes and sacralizes bonding in matrimony, nourishing in Eucharist, the healing and anointing, the forgiving and reconciliation, so that our Sacraments are fulfilling of the kind of strength and support that families find in loving one another and in establishing community among themselves.

The popes have said that "the home is the domestic Church": that we are the Church. Discuss the relationship of Church, institutional, and family. Talk about how family feeds the Church and how Church necessarily feeds family. If we're not Church at home, we can't be Church when we go to church. If we are not family, we can't become Church.

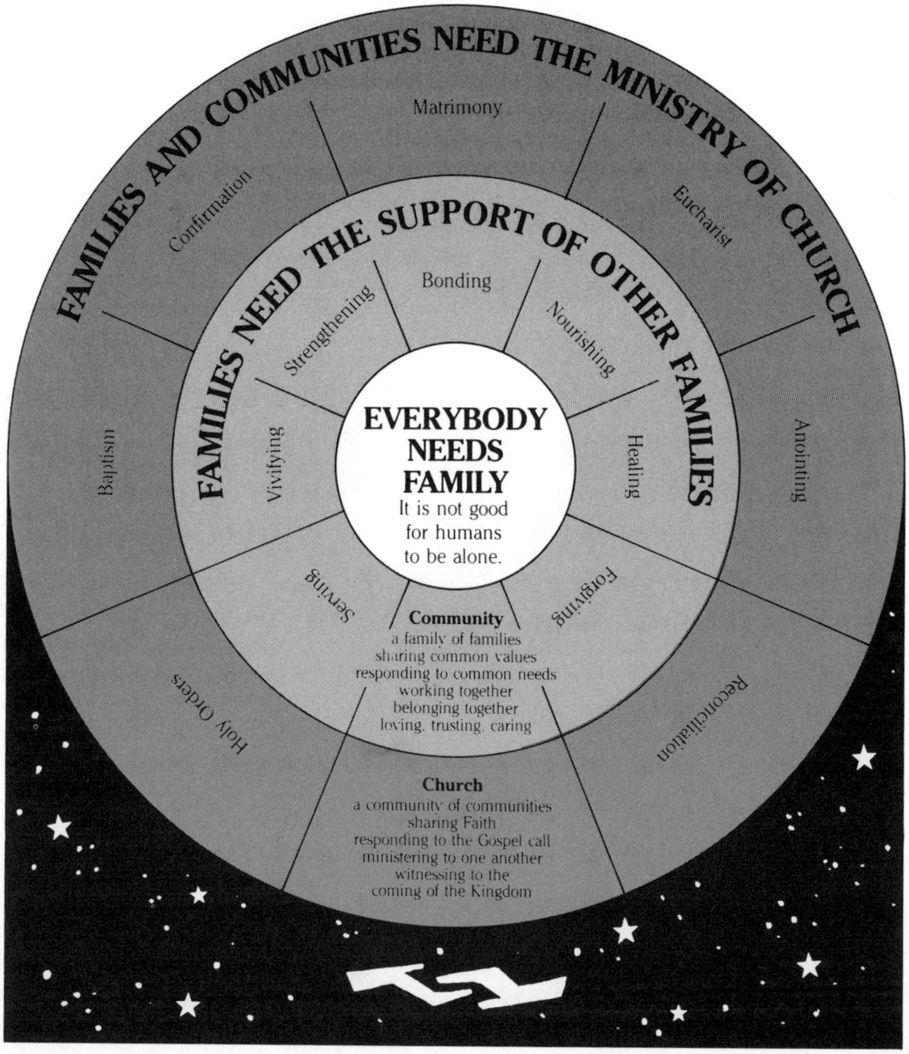

Diagram of Shared Faith, Values, Love

Sr. THEA BOWMAN, FSPA, Ph.D.

Children close to the heart of
Family
Community
Church
respond and remain constant to the VALUES of
Family
Community
Church.

Look at the word *family* at the bottom of the diagram below. See how the life of community and Church radiate from family. If we nurture faith, values, and love in the family, then we can nurture faith, values, and love in the community and the Church.

Traditions and rituals that embody that faith, values, and love have to be worked on, and so we have family histories, memories, prayer, and catechesis, and celebrations as well as family dreams, goals, and plans. In faith we remember our history; we remember that we've come this far by faith. We celebrate that faith in our liturgies. We pass on our values when we dream and plan and work together. We celebrate the love we bear for one another in family fun, being together, enjoying one another, and in family ministry. We minister to our family, we minister within our family, we minister within the Black community. We, as Church, minister to our brothers and sisters, wherever we find them.

Family is the basic raw material from which community and Church can be formed. Family is the model of Church.

Discuss how traditions and rituals of family, community, and Church embody faith, values, and love and provide life-giving connection with our past, vitality and comfort for our present, and hope and courage for our future.

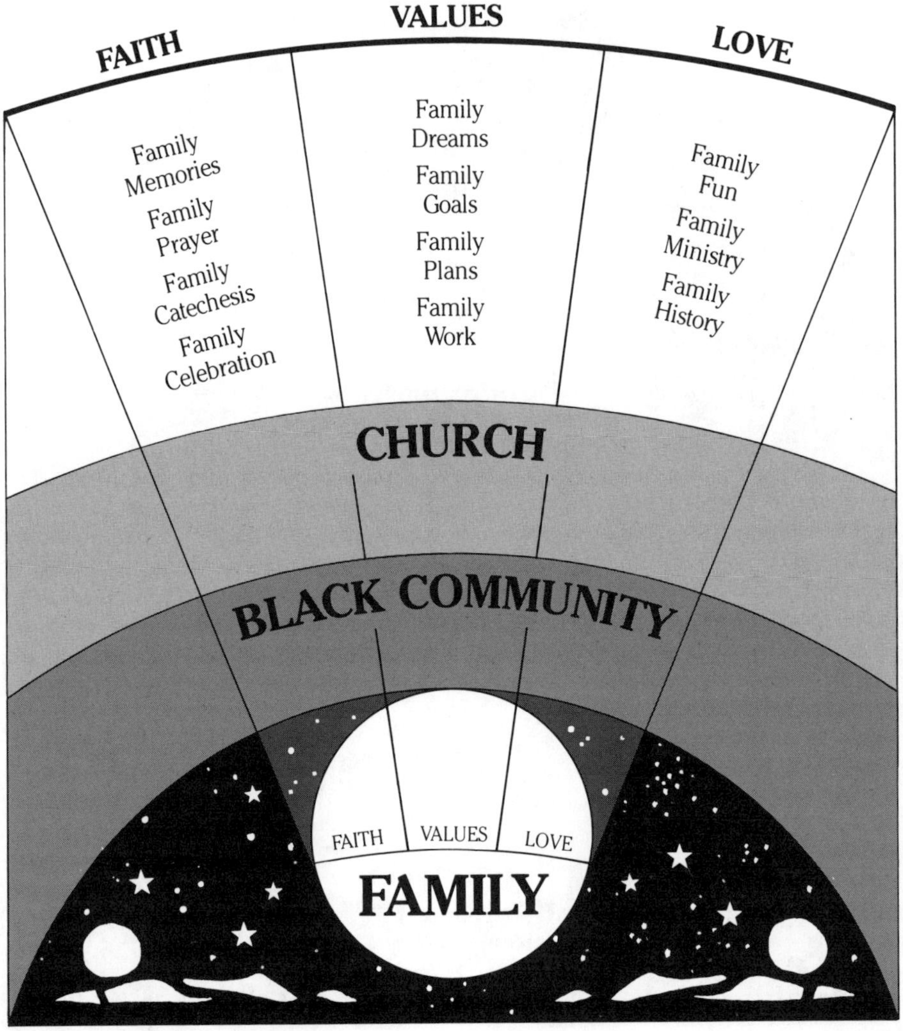

The Gift of Being Black and Catholic

Fr. Clarence Jos. Rivers, Jr., Ph.D.

"Blessed be the Lord
who has given such gifts to his people!
Not a single word has gone unfulfilled
of the entire generous promise
made to our foreparents."

God, who at sundry times and in diverse manners,
has spoken in times past,
today has spoken to us
in the example that Paul gives in his letter to the Corinthians,
in the example of the wise King Solomon,
and in the words of Jesus addressed to the man whom he had healed.

When Paul wrote to the church at Corinth,
he addressed a church with profound problems;
a church beset with bickering and fissured into factions,
with only a fumbling grasp on its beliefs,
unsure and shaky in its morals.
And yet, Paul's very first emotion for this church
is not anxiety and anguish over its turmoil,
but gratitude for its gifts.
The very first characteristic of this church that Paul focuses on
is that this church has been blessed with the gifts of the Spirit.

And as Solomon stood before the newly erected edifice
that was the very first temple that Israel had built for Yahweh,
this wise man must have known
that this throng gathered before him from the Twelve Tribes,
though united for the moment,
would sooner or later be splintering apart once again.
But Solomon must also have known the wisdom of counting one's blessings;
for he cries out, not trumpeting his troubles,
not burdening his people with his fears,
but baring his grateful soul to them in a song of praise, exclaiming:
"Blessed be the Lord who has given such gifts to his people!"

And so, with such inspiration,
even though fully aware of the growing pains
that beset our young black Catholic movement within the church,
we dare today to focus
not on our problems but on the unique blessings that are ours,
blessings that are bestowed on us
not only for our own sake but for the sake of all people.
Today we reflect not on the fact that we have problems
but on the fact that we may very well be the God-given solution to some problems.

Just as we believe that God has called us,
has given us a vocation,
not only as individual persons but also as a collective people,
even as he called Abraham and his descendants,
so too must we believe
that God has promised us special gifts to carry out our vocation
so that through us all the nations of the earth may be blessed.
And so, it may be asked,
what are our special gifts?

First, we are blessed ourselves
and we are a blessing to the society in which we live
because we are *both* black and Catholic.

Fr. Clarence Jos. Rivers, Jr., Ph.D., priest of the Archdiocese of Cincinnati, musician, playwright, and dramatist, is president of Stimuli, Inc., a company which adopts the performing and visual arts to the needs of more effective worship and education. He is author of several books including *Reflections, Soulfull Worship* and *The Spirit in Worship.* Fr. Rivers launched a revolution in church music with *An American Mass Program.* He lectures widely in North America, Europe, and Africa and is a founding member of the North American Academy of Liturgy and the Martin Luther King Fellows. He served for several years as a board member of the Liturgical Conference.

Rogelio Solis/Courtesy of Mississippi Today

Father George Clements, with a prophet's perception,
pointed out several years ago
that black Catholics might be a pivotal point in American society.
The fabric of our cities,
already weakened by economic decay,
stands ready to be torn apart
because of the tensions
that exist between the major elements of those cities,
namely the black population
and its chief rivals, ethnic white, predominately Catholic groups.
Conceivably, we might walk and talk on common grounds with both groups.
On the one hand we might be able to walk and talk
with many of those white groups
because we share with them the common ground of the Roman church;
and we might be able to walk and talk
with black groups
because we share with them the common ground of blackness
and the common cause of black liberation.
Conceivably, then, we can be a thread
to mend the torn fabric of our society.
and therefore we can be a blessing to this society.
"Blessed be the Lord who has given such gifts to his people!"

We are also blessed because we are Catholic
and as such we have inherited a rich treasury of ritual
so appealing to the religious sensibilities,
so appealing to the sacramental sense, the ritual sense
of our brothers and sisters of African descent in the black Protestant churches,
but so lacking to them in most of the Protestant traditions.
We are preserving for them a sacramental heritage,
just as they are preserving for us the heritage of soul, the treasure of negritude.
And now we are at the point in history
where each group of us is beginning to realize
what value we are to one another.
"Blessed be the Lord who has given such gifts to his people!"

Finally, and most importantly,
we are blessed because we are black
and as such have immediate access to the gift of negritude,
the gift of blackness, the gift of soul.
This gift is no simple thing.
It is a manifold gift, a many-faceted jewel.
It is a cultural thrust
which facilitates not only the way
that we excel in the arts of singing and dancing and praying and preaching,
but also enables us to relate humanely to God,
and helps us to live in harmony,
in a nonexploitive way with all of God's world.

Specifically because it facilitates soulfulness,
and spiritual inspiration, and inspirational celebration,
negritude is a gift that could greatly bless the worshiping church.
Indeed it is a grace that the worshiping church desperately needs.
For, left to the devices of Euro-American culture,
the cultural thrust of so-called Western Civilization,
the worship of the church will not be adequately revitalized
no matter how much mere structural reform is done.
For you cannot discursively think your way,
nor technologically and historically structure your way into vital worship,
into dynamic religious celebration.
While the thrust of Euro-American culture is indeed a good thing,
it is not a universal medicine
to be prescribed for any and every ill of the body of society.
It is a cultural thrust that tends to be discursive, and technological and analytical

and is inevitably given to defining everything, including God,
who is undefinable!
This analytical and discursive tendency
is the strength of Western culture,
but it is at the same time, its weakness.
For example, at its heights, epitomized in its universities,
Western culture strangely places more value on scholarly explanations of humor
than it does on the art of telling jokes;
more value on studying and talking about things than on doing things.
That is why its schools produce students who can define the parts of speech
but who cannot write decent sentences;
that is why they produce thousands of literary critics
who claim to know the rules of drama,
but not even a handful of playwrights
who can apply the rules and turn out plays that really move people.

And this is why, even within the worshiping church,
which is virtually a prisoner of the Western academic tradition,
we are most frequently appointed to ministerial positions
for our administrative skills and sometimes for our discursive theological abilities;
but not for our worship skills,
not for our grasp of the cultic arts
of preaching and praying and presiding at worship and leading people in song.
This is why we produce theologians and catechists who can explain the faith,
but no poets who can revel in the faith.
We produce scholars who can critique the Psalms of David,
but produce no modern Davids to create Psalms today.
We produce no inspiring preachers to make the word of God live,
no prophets whose burning words
can transform our cold hearts of stone into warm hearts of flesh,
no ministers whose skills with words of prayer
can give heaven-bent wings to the heavy thoughts that anchor our hearts to the ground.

This is why the average Catholic church-goer
who has been exposed only to Euro-American church culture,
seldom dreams of being inspired, or of being spiritually uplifted at Mass.
This is why the average Catholic church-goer
neither expects nor asks anything from Sunday worship
except that it be not-too-long.
And this is why the departure from the church after Sunday Mass
is one of the fastest movements in the life of the average Catholic!

This is also why reform in worship has replaced unintelligible Latin,
which nobody understood,
with bland, insipid, and tasteless English
that nobody wants to listen to;
and why the sluggishly played organ
has all too frequently been replaced by the pitifully plunked guitar;
and why the avant-garde manifestations of contemporary suburban Christian celebration
sometimes comes down to a dependence on gimmicks
like butterfly banners for Easter Sunday
and helium filled balloons for Ascension Thursday;
and this is sadly why the average Catholic congregation
is so much like Ezekiel's vision of a stagnant sprawl of dry and lifeless bones
lacking the breath of the Spirit.

Now this is a problem.
But we praise God today
because he has given us a solution to this problem.
We praise God today
because he has blessed us with the gift of negritude
and has made it possible for us to be channels of that Spirit,
which can restore life to our dead worship.
Our cultural heritage, as seen in the dominance of black culture
in the world of popular culture;

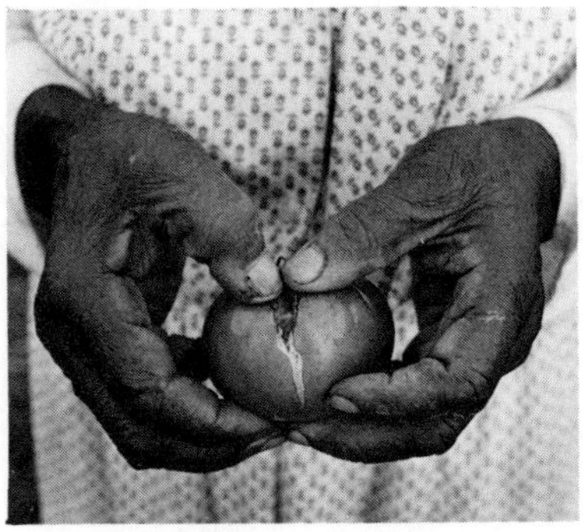
Rogelio Solis/Courtesy of Mississippi Today

and most especially,
our cultural heritage as experienced
in the moving, inspiring, soulful, spiritual worship
of the traditional black churches,
is a sacrament of the Spirit to bring life to dry bones.
"Blessed be the Lord who has given such gifts to his people!"
Not a single word has gone unfulfilled
of the entire generous promise made to our foreparents
that through them and their descendants
all the nations of the earth would be blessed!
Saint Paul might well address us today
with the words of gratitude
that he addressed to the church at Corinth:
Christ has been so confirmed among us
that we lack no spiritual gifts,
so that we lack no gift of the Spirit,
so that we lack no soul.
Thank God for the favor he has bestowed on us
in Christ Jesus, in whom we have been richly endowed
with every gift of knowledge and speech,
and every gift of understanding
and the power of soulful expression
to communicate that understanding.
"Blessed be the Lord who has given such gifts to his people!"
Let us go home to our families and friends,
and make it clear to them
how much the Lord in his loving kindness has done for us!

Intended from the outset to underline the possibility of being both authentically Black and authentically Catholic, significant works of Stimuli Inc., are unique among the resources cited and/or quoted here. Fr. Clarence Jos. Rivers, Jr., Ph.D., founded Stimuli Inc., to apply the arts to the needs of education, religious, and civic rituals; and to foster humane moral growth among peoples through the arts. *The Spirit in Worship* and *Soulfull Worship*, two inseparable volumes, have been critically acclaimed for their authentic synthesis of cultures. This two-volume set contains imaginative and authoritative inquiries into the basis of cultures and is of particular interest to *anyone* examining the language, literature, communicative styles, and psychology of both the African and European Churches. Fr. Rivers and his associates are available for workshops, lectures, consultations, and performances. Stimuli plans, produces, and oversees (1) ritual ceremonies, dramas, readings; (2) artwork, ritual objects, and vesture. Moreover, Stimuli invites special commissions in music, educational projects, and research papers. Their specialty has been demonstrating and teaching the "how" of creating effective, inspiring, and converting worship. All inquiries are welcome. Contact Stimuli Inc., Fr. Clarence Jos. Rivers, Jr., President, 17 Erkenbrecher Ave., Cincinnati, Ohio 45220-2202. Phone: 513/221-3889 or 221-5538.

Speak the Truth to the People

MARI EVANS, Ph.D.

Speak the truth to the people
Talk sense to the people
Free them with reason
Free them with honesty
Free the people with Love and Courage and Care for their Being
Spare them the fantasy
Fantasy enslaves
A slave is enslaved
Can be enslaved by unwisdom
Can be enslaved by black unwisdom
Can be reenslaved while in flight from the enemy
Can be enslaved by his brother whom he loves
His brother whom he trusts
His brother with the loud voice
And the unwisdom

Speak the truth to the people
It is not necessary to green the heart
Only to identify the enemy
It is not necessary to blow the mind
Only to free the mind
To identify the enemy is to free the mind
A free mind has no need to scream
A free mind is ready for other things
To BUILD black schools
To BUILD black children
To BUILD black minds
To BUILD black love
To BUILD black impregnability
To BUILD a strong black nation
To BUILD.

Speak the truth to the people.
Spare them the opium of devil-hate.
They need no trips on honky-chants.
Move them instead to a BLACK ONENESS.
A black strength which will defend its own
Needing no cacophony of screams for activation.
A black strength which attacks the laws
exposes the lies disassembles the structure
and ravages the very foundation of evil.

Speak the truth to the people
To identify the enemy is to free the mind
Free the mind of the people
Speak to the mind of the people
Speak Truth.

CHD/Peter Magubane

"Speak the Truth to the People," Mari Evans, from *I Am a Black Woman*, published by William Morrow & Company, 1970. Used by permission of the author.

Mari Evans, Ph.D., assistant professor at the African Studies and Research Center of Cornell University, Ithaca, New York, is author of *I Am a Black Woman* and *Nightstar.* Editor of *Black Women Writers 1950–1980* (Doubleday), Dr. Evans has been on the faculties of Indiana, Purdue, and Northwestern Universities.

Black Families in Perspective

ANDREW BILLINGSLEY, PH.D.

When we think of Black families, we must think of very strong bonds of kinship. For the concept of family, of belonging to the same closely related unit, is deeply ingrained in the Black experience.

Thus, whether we think of our African background, where family life was the central feature of community and national life; or whether we think of slavery, where even during that reign of terror many of our people held fast to the notion of belonging together even when separated; or whether we think of modern times, when the forces of racism, poverty, and violence often keep us apart, the spirit of family is still strong among us. It has never died out. The family thus represents a most important aspect of the struggle of our people for survival. And, it has been the family more than any other institution which has helped our people to survive, to find meaning in life, and to reach remarkable levels of achievement.

The study of Black family life in America is one approach to the set of hard questions we are asking ourselves these days; namely, "Who are we as a people?" "Where did we come from?" "Where are we going?" It is our view that Black families are among the strongest and most resilient institutions in the nation. Were it not so, we would not have survived as a people, and the national society would be even more inhuman and inhumane than it is.

This view is strikingly different from the more typical view of Black families that one finds in most literature. The typical view and analysis of research data begin with the idea and conclude with the opinion that Black families are weak, matriarchal, unstable, and make no substantial contribution to Black people or the nation. Our view is just the opposite. It grows out of not only personal experience and observation, but also out of considerable research and analysis of the research of other scholars. Our view is most consistent with that of a relatively new stream of Black scholarship exhibited by such students of family life as Hylan Lewis, Alvin Poussaint, St. Clair Drake, Camille Jeffers, Robert Staples, Joyce Ladner Carrington, Robert Hill, and a new breed of young Black scholars who have cast off the old white-racist-oriented concept of Black families as deviant, and have come to view Black family life, in its own right, as a source and reflection of Black culture and Black consciousness. . . .

BLACK CULTURE

In a very real sense, the question whether or not Black culture exists pales into meaninglessness when we reflect seriously on the fact and the meaning of family life among Black people. Culture refers to the totality of the ways of life of a people. It includes the basic conditions of our existence, our behavior, style of life, values, preferences, and the creative expressions that emanate from our work and play. It is, in short, the way we live and have our being. There can be little doubt that the ways of life for Black folks in America are different in major respects from the ways of white folks. There are similarities, too. But the repository for the culture of a people is the family, and in the Black family resiliency, adaptability, and sheer strength are primarily responsible for the fact that we as Black people have survived at all in this alien and hostile land. The heroic struggles of the Black man to hold his head high, protect his loved ones, and fight off the forces who would oppress him at every turn have not been sufficiently appreciated in the writings about our people, and in the textbooks that all schoolchildren use to learn. Much of this heroism has been expressed and lived out within the intimate set of relationships which is the family.

The role of the Black woman has received more attention in considerations of the family; but even here, most of what we read about the Black woman is written by people who do not understand or care about her real triumphs and tragedies, her joys and sorrows. Yet the Black woman in America

Andrew Billingsley, Ph.D., is professor of sociology and Afro-American studies at the University of Maryland. A former president of Morgan State University in Baltimore, he was visiting scholar and professor of social welfare at the Institute for the Study of Social Change of the University of California, Berkeley. His extensive writing includes the influential *Black Families in White America* (Prentice-Hall), *Children of the Storm* (Harcourt, Brace) and *Black Families and the Struggle for Survival* (Friendship Press). Articles by Dr. Billingsley have appeared in many professional publications, and he has testified on behalf of families before congressional committees.

has surely withstood, endured, and overcome much more oppression than any other segment of the national population. Still she remains at the bottom of the ladder of economic and political power. In the realm of the overall culture, however, she continues to reign supreme. For she continues to be the major creator, transmitter, and repository of the cultural heritage of our people and the major source of socialization, guidance, and inspiration for our children. All this is done best in the intimate setting of the family.

Or, consider the life and times of the Black child. There can hardly be any more severe handicaps in this country than being born poor and Black. To survive at all is a triumph. To survive with a sense of optimism, faith, and commitment to life that keeps one out of trouble most of the time and enables one to contribute to the welfare of the community is even more miraculous. These are miracles performed regularly by the overwhelming majority of Black children and youth. And in the realm of creativity, whether in religion, music, art, literature, education, or politics, Black youth are surely the nation's leading culture producers.

So. Black family life and Black culture are so heavily interrelated that it is hard to think of one without the other. It is well to keep this interrelationship in mind when studying about Black families, their trials and tribulations as well as their problems and their promises; their tragedies and their triumphs; their ups and their downs.

In contemporary discussions of Black culture, there are two types of culture which are often used interchangeably and sometimes without a recognition of their distinction. One type of culture refers to what might be considered the "artistic expressions of a people." This includes art, drama, literature, entertainment, music, and the like. This is quite distinct from the other type of culture which refers to how a people live. The first type of culture may be considered "entertainment culture." The second type may be considered "survival culture," for it includes the patterned ways of surviving, living, and ways of doing things. This is also the type of culture described and studied by anthropologists and sociologists. The distinction between the two types is critical. Even when one or the other of these general types of culture is being considered, there are important subtypes and dimensions in each as well as important and differing conceptions.

CHD/Peter Magubane

Part of the debate about the existence of Black culture is based on differing conceptions of culture as the way of life of a people. One view of culture looks for unique and perhaps exotic artifacts; the other view looks toward the more basic patterns of behavior and values of a people. The existence and importance of Black culture does not depend, however, on its differences from other people. Its existence depends simply on its own reality; its importance depends on its functions; that is to say, its consequences for the life and death of Black people. The nature of the separate world within which Black people and white people live as well as the nature of Black culture itself must be subjected to vigorous, critical, and continuous examination and discussion so that we all come to understand it better.

If our culture is unique, complex, rich, and distinctive, it is, in part, because we are the sum total of our experience, and our experience as a people stems from at least four major sources. We are first and foremost an African people. Our African heritage has not been blotted out by our experience since leaving the continent. It shows in our physical features which help to condition how we behave and how we view ourselves. More important, our African features heavily influence how others view us and behave toward us. They are, therefore, a very important part of our contemporary culture. There are still strong among us not only physical similarities, but intellectual and common sensibilities; a sense of the importance of community, cooperation and the common good which is part of our African heritage. And beyond all that, there is that creative genius among us which expresses itself in both types of our culture. Whether in religion, music, literature, drama, dance, work and play, or in the more fundamental ways of surviving, we are coming increasingly to see that much of our African ways are still with us and have helped enable us to survive.

At the same time we are African, we are also an American people. Our culture has been shaped, in the large measure, by our history and experience in America. Thus, in being American, we are also, in part, a European people. The problem for us as Americans is that while we have been forced to adopt the language and life way of the American people in order first to serve them, and consequently to survive, we have nowhere been provided the same opportunities, privileges, or resources that other Americans enjoy. Consequently, beyond being an African people, and an American people, we are an Afro-American people. Our experience in America is not like that of any other group. And most of the contributions we have made both to entertainment culture and to survival culture have grown out of this fact, and each of these major streams of civilization—African, American and Afro-American—is complex and varied within itself. Each of them is also highly interrelated in our own experience. Houston Baker has described three major aspects in which Black culture is distinctive from white American culture.

First, he observes, we are an oral and musical people. Second, we have not succumbed to the individualistic ethos which is so much a part of the American character. We, as a people, are still more committed to a collective ethos which emphasizes the common good and common sharing. According to this view:

> Black society is not viewed as a protective arena in which the individual can work out his own destiny and gain a share of America's benefits by his own efforts. To the Black American these benefits are not attained solely by individual efforts alone, but by changes in the nature of society and the social, economic, and political advancement of a whole race of people.[1]

Finally, Baker emphasizes that because of the conditions under which we have lived in this country, much of our way of life is "repudiative." That is, we have developed the capacity and the necessity to repudiate much of what is the American way of life. And, because the American way of life is so inhuman, this critical capacity on our part is a highly valued aspect of our contribution to the nation. These three characteristics of our culture are only a beginning, for any group of Black people sitting around discussing our situation can come up with dozens of illustrations of the ways in which we are distinct people with a distinct anchor in history, and a distinct set of life conditions. Perhaps, the Black church on Sunday morning remains one of the most widespread evidences of our ancient and contemporary sense of Black peoplehood. And, indeed the Black family and the Black Church, as they have fortified each other down through the years, have helped to keep our people alive and strong and both realistic and optimistic at the same time.

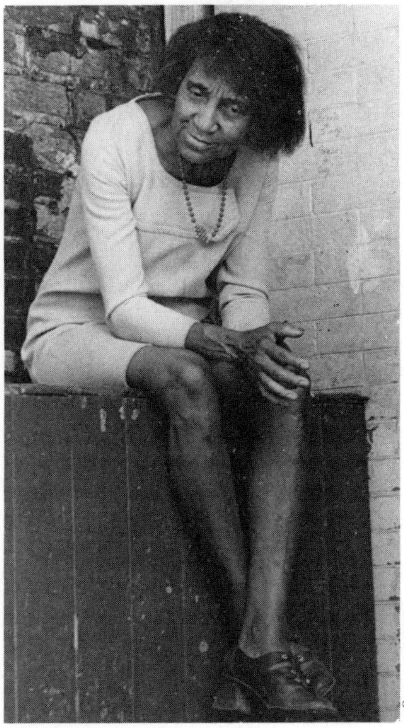
CHD/Dave Vaughn

NOTE

1. Houston Baker, "Completely Well: One View of Black American Culture," in *Key Issues in the Afro-American Experience* vol. 1 (New York: Harcourt, Brace, Jovanovich, 1971), 32.

The Black Family and the American Church

BISHOP EUGENE A. MARINO, SSJ, D.D.

THE CHALLENGE OF DEFINITION

Attempts to examine the true meaning of the black family, its power and solidarity, and the context of strengths and weaknesses within which it functions, have frequently foundered on the reef of erroneous presuppositions and misleading statistics. Any analysis of the black family must be careful to distinguish the historical conditions that existed in the first half of the nineteenth century from those that have been present in the last half of the twentieth century. There are elements both of continuity and discontinuity. Many of the social patterns of the slavery era are still apparent. Other aspects of slavery have faded into the dim recesses of a dark past. We must avoid the pitfall of assuming that present realities can be projected backwards to explain the nature of family relationships in the nineteenth century.

Rogelio Solis/Courtesy of Mississippi Today

An illustration of an abiding reality which reflects the continuity of experience from African heritage, and the days of slavery, to the present can be found in the development of patterns of mutual aid within the black family.

Economic pressures have affected this mutual-aid system in a paradoxical manner. On the one hand, it was because of extreme privation and the circumstances brought about by slavery that black familes carried on their African family traditions and forged solid bonds of support within their ranks. And yet, the continuing impact of stubborn poverty now exerts a powerful strain on those bonds, even to the point of destroying them in families made desperate by a seemingly inescapable cycle of poverty.

One of the most important factors bearing upon the present status of the black family is the population shift into the big cities that has taken place since the depression. In a thirty year period beginning in 1940, some 4 million blacks left rural areas and moved into cities.

This influx of blacks into the cities produced enormous problems of adjustment, the effects of which are still very much a part of urban life. Disruptive problems with poor housing, crime, the lack of quality education, and unemployment have troubled the inner cities of our nation in great measure because of the inability of the cities to absorb effectively such a large number of people, most of whom were unfamiliar with urban life. The fierce pressure of urban struggles with inadequate housing, inferior education, and massive unemployment has taxed the resources of the black family almost beyond endurance. But efforts to understand the scope and cause of urban problems have linked uncritically the social dysfunctions accompanying the population shift with the inherent structure of the black family. A monstrous confusion of causes with effects has jeopardized the progress gradually made by blacks in expressing their own understanding of the problems present. Black families have been approached as studies in pathologies. The effect of these analyses was to leave unfocused the time-proven resilience of the black family and to misconstrue the actual connection between urban poverty and black family patterns.

The allegation of black family disorganization frequently dominates any discussion of urban problems to the exclusion of larger social realities, such as massive structural unemployment, that are in fact responsible for the family problems perceived by researchers. Well-intentioned studies have often examined social problems in terms of color rather than income level, with the result that the findings are distorted by a conceptual flaw built into the research model.

In reaction to the pathology-disorganization approach of black family studies, some scholars have begun to stress the indigenous strengths of black family living. They have underscored the tremendous contribution of some im-

Bishop Eugene A. Marino, SSJ, D.D., an auxiliary bishop of the Archdiocese of Washington (D.C.), is regional bishop of the District of Columbia and Montgomery County, Maryland. Ordained as a member of the Society of St. Joseph, he was elected its vicar general in 1971. Prior to that he was spiritual director at St. Joseph's Seminary in Washington, D.C.

portant and enduring strengths such as the adaptability of family roles, a high orientation toward achievement in varied fields, the strong kinship bonds that successfully blunted the oppressive force of slavery, and a firm religious orientation.

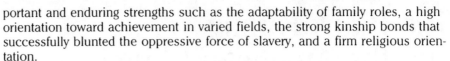

CHD/Michal Heron

As we observe the sharply contrasting conclusions reached by different social scientists, we realize that it is imperative all the more to refrain from facile generalizations about the nature of black family living in the United States. The corollary of this realization is that the Church must work actively to correct popular misconceptions about black families, some of which are based on misinformation, while other such misconceptions are simply the veneer of a pervasive, if subtle, racism. The Church must oppose at every juncture the attempt to define black people as a "problem" requiring a "solution" rather than as uniquely graced members of the human family who have made substantive contributions to the building of this country and to its defense for centuries. When we reflect, for example, upon the impact of black labor in the agricultural growth of the country, the sweat and labor that so often provided food and cotton for an expanding nation, we can appreciate the horrendous irony of treating the struggle of this heroic people as a problem defined by less than sympathetic observers.

In a special way we must be conscious of the irreparable injury done to young people when they are portrayed as social problems to be dealt with rather than as individuals who are encouraged to dream of the future and to work toward the attainment of those dreams.

Another distortion occurs when only one model, that of the nuclear family, is gratuitously used as a basis for evaluation of the black family. Evidence exists that a different family pattern has emerged within the black community as a response to traditions, economic pressures, and social realities. The extended-family model more accurately describes the family reality that evolved within the black community. The black extended family has been remarkably adept at promoting the welfare of dependent family members, in dealing with crisis situations, in providing for the necessities of life and a general sense of economic security. In short, the extended-family model evolved as a survival mechanism and continues to promote familial and social cohesion.

The black extended family has been described as "a multigenerational, interdependent kinship system which is welded together by a sense of obligation to relatives; is organized around a 'family base' household; is generally guided by a 'dominant family figure'; extends across geographical boundaries to connect family units to an extended family network; and has a built-in mutual aid system for the welfare of its members and the maintenance of the family as a whole." Such a family model would be ignored by the conventional view that the nuclear family constitutes the norm for all races in the United States.

CONSIDERATION FOR PROGRAM PLANNING

The Catholic Church in the United States has historically demonstrated a willingness to support its values and convictions with programmatic action. What are the needs to be addressed?

THE NEED FOR DIALOGUE

The Church can make a significant contribution to the growth of the black family by fostering a dialogue with the larger white community to communicate the real needs of black Americans, and to underscore the duty of society to respect the rights and legitimate aspirations of blacks and other minorities.

Discrimination against blacks in jobs, housing, and education still persists as an obstacle to the integrity of black family life.

VALUES

The Church can speak with a unique credibility to the need for enduring values that support family solidarity and growth. A fundamental shift has taken place in American society in the direction of a secular philosophy that disparages older values of duty, discipline, filial devotion, and the work ethic which have influenced the living patterns of families in general—black, white, and Hispanic. We must recognize the deleterious impact upon our youth of irresponsible sexual mores that are developing in a permissive society, and the rampant materialism of a society whose values are sharply at variance with the values of mutual aid and human generosity that grew in slavery and still remain as part of a profound religious faith in the black community.

UNEMPLOYMENT

The black community faces the prospect of severe, unyielding economic dislocation because of the impact of unemployment. Much of the unemployment has been due to cynical neglect and planned anti-inflationary measures. The resulting economic dysfunction is perpetuating poverty to an intolerable degree. It is virtually institutionalizing correlative problems of crime, suicide, mental illness, and alcoholism. Teen-age unemployment in particular is epidemic, averaging more than 50 percent of the number of eligible black teenagers in many of our cities. Assuredly, we acknowledge that there is no panacea for this shattering dislocation of social energy and personal self-esteem. But we must not shrink from the challenge because of its magnitude.

AFFIRMATIVE ACTION

In the wake of the *Bakke* decision handed down by the Supreme Court, courts across the land will be struggling to rule on the nature and scope of racial discrimination in education and other fields. We must speak with one prophetic voice about the need to remain faithful to the Civil Rights Acts of the 1960s—their spirit and their enactments. To renege on their pledge of equal citizenship would be tragedy of unparalleled proportions.

EDUCATION

As we approach the twenty-fifth anniversary of the *Brown* v. *Board of Education* decision of the Supreme Court, we are painfully conscious of the limited success of desegregation. The busing controversy has rubbed raw the deepest nerves of American society. We must not relax our vigilance in seeing that black youngsters have the opportunity of receiving quality education and if they so desire, in a truly integrated setting. Quality education is a necessary precondition for economic sufficiency which, in turn, is a major contributory factor in family stability.

USCC/Lou Niznik

HOUSING

An issue of immense significance confronts our cities in the matter of equitable housing. When we study the origins of present housing patterns that divide the inner cities from the suburbs, we can observe the fact that the availability of mortgages in the aftermath of World War II was greatly instrumental in enabling citizens to finance homes otherwise beyond their means. Many of those homes are in communities that we now recognize as suburbia. For the most part, these suburbs have not been available to blacks. The net result has been a limited supply of decent housing for black families. The inner cities, where many black people have found residence, are sorely in need of the same kind of federal assistance that created our suburbs.

At the same time, efforts must be undertaken to secure an adequate supply of decent housing for black families where, without discrimination, they can pursue the fulfillment of their familial responsibilities.

CRIME

A pervasive element of our social fabric today is the problem of crime. An otherwise sophisticated society is only beginning to realize the extent of crime. Within this larger picture of an unprincipled and increasingly hedonistic society, seized with a compulsion for unending acquisitions, the most severe penalties for criminal conduct have been exacted, often unfairly, against black Americans. A disproportionate number of black men spend useless lives behind prison bars. The Church must function as the voice of the tired, the demoralized, and the victimized—those against whom our criminal justice system has aimed its harshest sanctions. The Church should ask for a reexamination of dysfunctional aspects of our criminal justice procedures, especially where these procedures adversely affect the family life of the poor and minorities.

THEOLOGICAL REFLECTIONS

The experience of the black family in our nation is a genuine focal point for several salient theological reflections. They are touched by a deep reservoir of hope, for the pages of our history offer unchallenged evidence that in some magnificent way the gentle grace of the Spirit has sustained life in our families when only death beckoned. That Spirit of the Lord nourished the spirits of black parents and their children when the lash of the whip and the noose of the lynch mob were cruel instruments of daily terror.

The black family has been a sign of transcendence in the fact that it has consistently realized and affirmed the deepest yearnings of the human spirit. No charts or tracts existed to explain the experience of slavery. There were no role models present, to render the lash less stinging. It was imperative to recognize and affirm the identity—needs, goals, dreams, fears—of one another in a totally new environment, without the guidance of known mentors. Yet the needed affirmation of shared faith and personhood took place, gradually, firmly, ineluctably. The black family has never viewed its historical deprivations as an estrangement from the Lord. Rather, the experience of suffering has brought to the fore an attunement to the Lord's kindness that in turn generated a sense of certain survival, a determination to "make it" against all odds. By affirming the presence of God in their midst, the black family has at the same time affirmed its most noble aspirations of communal love and solidarity whose patterns continue as mutual aid.

Finally, the black family contributed to a view of the Church that is fundamentally Christocentric. The Church could never be understood except as a congregation of believers who shared the sufferings of a crucified Lord and who assembled on solemn occasions to renew their link with the mystery of Christ's presence. At the promulgation of the Emancipation Proclamation, the black leaders of this nation could be found in Washington, D.C., in genuine celebration, in a church at midnight, ushering in their hard-won freedom in the presence of the Lord who had made it all possible. This awareness of an intrinsic connection between the Church and the Lord that it worshiped is yet another facet of this sign of transcendence, the black family in the United States.

Rogelio Solis/Courtesy of Mississippi Today

A Black Christian Perspective of Spirituality

FR. ALBERT M. MCKNIGHT, CSSP

Black Spirituality must encompass morals, which are those practiced values that greatly influence our behavior and attitudes toward each other and toward our environment. The development of the spiritual life involves the practice of values which will supplant the prevalent oppressive values of individualism, dog-eat-dog competition, anything for money, and materialistic consumerism, which we have adopted wholesale.

The Nguzo Saba, as developed by Maulana Ron Karenga, provide a practicable alternative.

The Seven Principles are

1. *Umoja*, unity: To strive for and maintain unity in the family, community, nation, and race.
2. *Kujichagulia*, self-determination: To define ourselves, create for ourselves, and speak for ourselves.
3. *Ujima*, collective work and responsibility: To build and maintain our community together and make our brothers' and sisters' problems our problems and to solve them together.
4. *Ujamaa*, familyhood and cooperative economics: *Familyhood* means to extend to all our people the respect and cooperation due brothers and sisters. *Cooperative* means to work together in peace and harmony. *Economics* is the ownership, production, distribution, and consumption of goods and services. *Cooperative economics* is the establishment and ownership of business on a one-member, one-vote basis with limited dividends on investments and patronage return. We must build and maintain our own stores, shops, and other businesses and profit from them together.
5. *Nia*, purpose: Our purpose is to work together and struggle together for the unification, liberation, and independence of all people of African descent, especially those in the South, by gaining, maintaining, and using power.
6. *Kuumba*, creativity: To do always as much as we can in the way we can in order to leave our community more beautiful and beneficial than we inherited it. The old ways have not worked. We must create new ways to struggle for unity, liberation, and independence.
7. *Imani*, faith: To believe with all our hearts in our parents, our teachers, our leaders, our people, and the righteousness and victory of our struggle. We believe in African people and the Nguzo Saba. We believe that we can and must do the impossible (i.e., to unify, liberate, and free all people of African descent).

The words used to describe the Nguzo Saba Seven Principles are from the Kiswahili language. Kiswahili is an African language that is nontribal (i.e., it is spoken by people of several different tribes and was developed so that people of different language backgrounds could communicate with each other). Therefore, Kiswahili itself implies the principle of Umoja—unity. Using Kiswahili to describe a Black value system is also appropriate because it exemplifies the principle of Kujichagulia—self-determination. We are using a language created by Africans, for Africans, to describe a moral code designed for Africans. In rejecting a European language, we are establishing a separate and distinct identity and direction for ourselves. Kiswahili puts us in touch with ourselves and our past, giving us a strong foundation to face our present struggle.

In addition to the Seven Principles, there are Twenty-one Complements to the Nguzo Saba which act as a guide for daily living.

1. Always strive for greater degrees of unity in the family among our people and our allies.
2. Always show bold initiatives in all we do.

Fr. Albert M. McKnight, CSSp, is pastor of Holy Ghost Church in Opelousas, Louisiana. He serves as president of the Southern Cooperative Development Fund, vice-chairperson of the National Consumer Coop Bank, and chairperson of the Consumer Cooperative Development Corporation, all headquartered in Lafayette, Louisiana.

3. Always share work and responsibility consciously and collectively.
4. Always share what we have with those who share our values and aspirations for a better world and way to live.
5. Always dare greatness for the community and our people.
6. Always work to make the lives of our people better and more beautiful.
7. Always love and believe in our people and involve ourselves profoundly and firmly in their lives.
8. Always speak the truth and call things by their right name.
9. Always move to broaden our base.
10. Always reach out to organize.
11. Always fight our fears and frustrations about what can't be achieved.
12. Always be audacious and honest in all we do.
13. Always remember we can always do more.
14. Cast aside cynicism, mysticism, and addiction to simple solutions.
15. Understand and appreciate the long time it takes to make progress and achieve victory.
16. Learn to struggle by struggling and studying struggle.
17. Work daily to overcome the negative attitudes, thoughts, and actions of ourselves and our people.
18. Learn tirelessly from everyone and everything and teach what we learn.
19. Hide no difficulties, failures, or mistakes and always encourage free, frank, and full discussions of issues.
20. Be humble in the admission of our mistakes and quick and thorough in the elimination of them.
21. Be patient and thorough in our work, conscious and committed in our struggle, terribly audacious in our example.

All our institutions (e.g., churches, schools, social clubs, fraternities, sororities, families, etc.) must work to guarantee the practice of these values. Otherwise, we are doomed to failure before we begin. Moral integrity guarantees the power to seek.

CHD/Michal Heron

"Black Christian Perspective of Spirituality," Albert M. McKnight, CSSp, from *Theology: A Portrait in Black*, Thaddeus J. Posey, OFM Cap, editor, copyright © 1980 National Black Catholic Clergy Caucus, Washington, D.C. Reprinted with permission.

Afrikan Love

HAKI R. MADHUBUTI A/K/A DON L. LEE

Our move is back toward the extended family, back toward the humanistic involvement of families with families, where no child is without a mother or father and no grandparent is without a son or daughter, where *all* is shared and we take care of each other. The basis of our family, as is our struggle, is *love*; the love of our children, the love of our ancestors, the love of our land, the love of the living Afrikans. That which harms a brother or sister in Zimbabwe should touch brothers and sisters in the diaspora. The extended-family concept is built around *human needs* and not the material needs of humans. In Swahili this concept of familyhood is called Ujamaa.

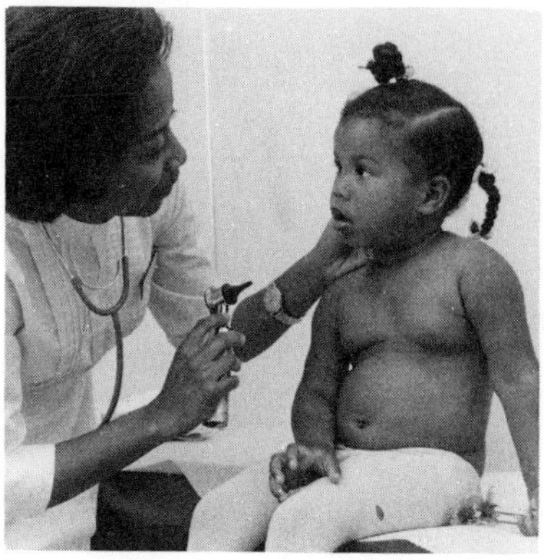

CHD/Michal Heron

Our selfishness and individualism is the cause for much of the cold in the Afrikan world today. We don't feel anymore. It seems as though all our energies are directed toward "making it." This is serious because it takes us away from the real problems and humanistic needs of the majority of the world's people. One of the methods that can be used for regaining the love we once had for each other is continuous and realistic *work* (Kazi) in the black community, especially with black children. If there is love in you, our children will bring it out. If there is no love in you, our children will make you feel some.

Our struggle should not be based upon the *hate* of anything, but the love of life and our people. If we have the necessary love, by definition we're automatically against anything that upsets our way of life and will fight to the *win*. One cannot build a movement on the negative. One cannot sustain a struggle on the anti. Our fight by definition should not be anti-European-Americans, anticapitalism or antiwhite, but should be pro-Pan-Afrikanism, pro-Ujamaa (co-operative economics) and pro-black people. This way we create a frame of reference whereas we are defining and acting in the positive rather than being defined by and reacting to the negative. By using our own frame of reference, we are giving alternative direction and introducing new values.

Nobody can define the needs of Afrikans but Afrikans. We don't see Afrikans in Sweden telling the Swedes how to run their lives! So, we too must define the direction that we must go ourselves. The Honorable Sekou Toure has stated: "You either serve the people or you use the people." There is no in-between. If genuine love exists and is passed on among our people, for a child to serve the community will not only be in keeping with the dictates of the black value system, but for the child, this would be an honor and privilege. This would be one of the ways that our sons and daughters acknowledge their thanks to their ancestors, their families and community for benefits that they enjoy in their youth and will continue to enjoy as they grow and mature.

The love that members of the Afrikan society reflect for the people of their society is something that is misunderstood and foreign to the European's way of life. It's like acupuncture is to the Western doctor. It cannot be co-opted and taught in eight easy lessons. So the AMA put a ban on it. The West has put a ban on Afrikans' getting together, thus aborting any love base to redevelop. Our love and responsibility to each other should be a way of life and must be taught from birth. The life style that we develop must be one of warmth and substance. Warmth: the ability to smile and touch the inner core of our people so as to radiate a sense of security, completeness and substance; the ability to offer a new reality, a new competence that successfully follows through on all projects; also, the ability to transmit within our world a feeling of confidence and security in our own worth and actions. . . .FRELIMO will regain their land because they generate warmth and substance in their daily fight. They are fighting *for* their people and, by definition, against their enemies—we accent the positive.

The love for our people should be so deep and clean that a verbalization of it becomes unnecessary, although at times expected. Our very actions, our life style must exemplify such a spirit. Our love must be so unshaking that it

Haki R. Madhubuti, who is also known as Don L. Lee, is director of Third World Press in Chicago.

stands the test of the European corruptibles: money, power, and sex. We must be so positive in our attitude toward each other that we never, never consciously or unconsciously, under any circumstances, take advantage of another brother or sister. I don't care if the niggers think that they are superslick! That's all right, because they're going to run up against the real-slick ones sooner or later. We must concentrate on the *positive*, on the constructive. Too often in our *blackness*, we're so bad that we scare our own people away. Our people fear us more than the white boy. We must be aware of this. There is an old Afrikan proverb that says "We must cure the illness without killing the patient." We are now at war for the minds of our people.

The relationship between man and man, man and woman, man and children will be clarified and redefined once the black man and woman involve themselves in the genuine struggle of the black world. As long as they remain apart from it, doing their *own* thang, by definition, *our* thang will never be completed.

The black woman to us is something extra special. Special, not in the sense that we should crown her queen and put her on a pedestal, but to understand that we have no future without her. She, as a complementary force working at our sides, reinforces us when we weaken and doubt the correctness of our struggle. The black woman and the black man should recognize that, in terms of tradition and family association, each has different roles to complete: a woman cannot be a father and a man cannot be a mother; they may substitute but will never fulfill those special roles.

At this time in our lives, we seem to be threatened by each other. That is to say that we've internalized the values and aspirations of our enemies to the point that our relationships with each other are sometimes strained and frustrating. The root of this is that we've become so acculturated to the European way of life that the changeover from Afrikan to European-American has left us very insecure as a people. We're so insecure in our manhood and womanhood that *a continuous reassertion* of a European individualism, vis-a-vis man and woman, inadvertently has made us antagonists. Black man against black man; black man against black woman; black woman against black woman; black woman against black man. All this stems from the European definition of man and woman which is based upon material possessions and superficial exterior rather than the human basis of Afrikan man and woman.

This is sad. Black men are being ripped off daily in the prisons and in numerous other death traps invented to separate us from the real world. It has been estimated that black women outnumber black men two and one-half to one and that dealing with that fact emotionally has driven black men and women further apart seeking answers where they cannot be found. You cannot solve a family problem when you're not even defined as a family.

The extended-family concept solves many problems. First, that of security. When one eats, all eat. If one has a house to live in, all have a house to live in. When one works, all who are physically able work. Most of the needs of the members of the family are met by the family—needs such as care for the aged, seeing that all children have a mother and father, quality education available for all the children and not just those who can afford such. This family structure allows you to pool your resources, thus making your bargaining power greater. For example, if there are fifty members in your community-family and if you got haircuts at a special barber shop, we're sure you could get a special rate; if all of the family members used a special cleaners for their clothing; again, a more economical rate. There are all kinds of possibilities in this and all kind of dangers if not operated within the correct value system and Afrikan frame of reference.

Basically, the extended family is the beginning of the extended organization. As with the family, a *new* and lasting trust is built which will enable its participants to function at the highest of their ability. This concept of shared and complementary work and study over that of personal possession and individual aggressiveness is the beginning of the solution to our many problems. Collective eating brings collective working; collective working brings collective thinking; collective thinking brings collective action; collective action brings results for the collective body. The future of our children is at stake.

catch that smile, return it
share that food, you've earned it
know your brother, build on it
help your sisters, make a way of life
of it
teach our children, by being it
create your life
around the love of it

"Afrikan Love," Haki R. Madhubuti a/k/a Don L. Lee, *From Plan to Planet*, copyright © 1973 Third World Press, Chicago. Reprinted with permission.

Rogelio Solis/Courtesy of Mississippi Today

PART IV

We Share

WE SHARE . . . FAITH

Faith has been the sustaining force of black life in America. The traditional black Church, with its emphasis on the saving presence of God throughout history, and on Christ as Liberator, has been the backbone of our constant struggle for freedom. That a people survive, grow, and indeed become strong despite their being the most frequent victims of unemployment, imprisonment, miserable housing, and the debilitating effects of drugs and disease, can only be a sign of the Spirit working among us.

Pope Paul VI
Black Perspectives on Evangelization in the Modern World

WE SHARE . . . FAITH

Family Activities

What is faith?

In what ways has faith sustained us as individuals? as family?

How has God manifested his saving presence in our lives as individuals? in our life as family?

How can we as family share faith? faith experiences? the faith journey? How can we plan for those kinds of sharing that will facilitate our growth together in faith?

How will we as family engage in the struggle for freedom?

Rogelio Solis/Courtesy of Mississippi Today

WE SHARE . . . VALUES

A Matter of Pride

SIDNEY B. SIMON, PH.D.

CHD/Franklin Williams

"Pride goeth before destruction, and a haughty spirit before a fall." The biblical injunction to avoid self-puffery is a valuable one. But unreasonable and unbridled pride is not what we are speaking of here.

Let the following situation define the right kind of pride. A family is sitting around the dinner table. As various courses are served, and interspersed with other conversations, each member of the family is asked to complete the sentence stem: "I am proud that. . . ." Perhaps that person will say, "I am proud that we all love each other," or "I am proud that we can all be together to share this meal," or "I am proud that we care about each other more than we care about material possessions," or "I am proud that my sisters and brothers are willing to share their problems with me." Sometimes, responses can be directed to a given category, for example, ecology, fighting racism, or sexism.

In this example of community or familial sharing, pride becomes part of a self-affirming ritual, almost a dinner table blessing. This is the kind of pride, of self-esteem, that this strategy encourages.

A Matter of Pride is a group activity. It can become an important part of your daily affirmation. Perhaps a family dinner table activity as described above.

You can't have a decent self-concept of who you are as a whole person without pride: Cherishing and prizing self is one of the criteria in defining self-values. False humility is as harmful as false pride. Be proud of what you do and what you are. Be willing to publicly affirm it. Regard your pride as a present to be shared.

A Matter of Pride will encourage you to do more things from which you can take pride. Think about what you have to be proud of in relation to some specific area or issue. It might be conservation or ecology, politics, social action, everyday activities, perhaps a demonstration of generosity of spirit or kindness.

People cannot be expected to be proud of everything they do or feel. But you should be able to define those things about which you feel good.

Sidney B. Simon, Ph.D., is a professor at the University of Massachusetts. A pioneer in the values-clarification movement, he is coauthor of five classic books: *Values and Teaching, Values Clarification, Meeting Yourself Half Way, Helping Your Child Learn Right from Wrong* and *The Ialac Story.* Dr. Simon conducts workshops and lectures throughout the world.

WE SHARE . . . VALUES

Pledge to the Afro-American Flag

I pledge allegiance to the destiny of Black people:
to the Red, Black, and Green.
I give my life and my love to my people.
I promise to keep an open mind toward all people
to seek the goals of unity and community,
to stand up for what is right
from now until Judgment Day! Right On!

Composed by 8th Grade Class of
Father Bertrand Elementary School
Memphis, Tennessee

AN ALTERNATIVE VERSION

I pledge allegiance to my black and Third World people.
I pledge to develop my mind and body to the greatest possible extent.
I will learn all that I can in order to give my best to my people in our struggle for liberation.
I will keep myself physically fit.
I will unselfishly share my knowledge and understanding with others in order to create a new and better world.
These principles I pledge to practice, thoughtfully, constructively, and daily in order to unite my people.

Recited by the Children of Resurrection School
Harlem, New York

Red symbolizes blood and suffering, redemption and liberty.
Black stands for the black peoples of the world.
Green is for hope and for the luxuriant fertility of our ancestral lands.

CHD/Barbara Baker Stephenson

WE SHARE . . . VALUES

Family Activities

I am proud that

We are proud that

Rogelio Solis/Courtesy of Mississippi Today

WE SHARE . . . LOVE

We Are All Refugees

Br. CYPRIAN LAMAR ROWE, FMS, Ph.D.

We are all refugees. We are seekers of a home that is just beyond our reach—a home for our hearts with their aspirations, a home for our minds with their staggering possibilities, a home for our bodies with their unceasing needs. Scripture tells us, indeed, about pilgrimages and "cities that are not lasting."

Our mission while we are here is to speak the words of hope to our fellow refugee-pilgrims. Our mission is to help them, by faith, to understand that we must be the door of Christ, opening out to the homeless—in whatever way they are homeless.

Much has been made of the response of Black people to the coming of the Southeast Asian (the Vietnamese). We have been accused of being selfish. We have been accused of refusing to empathize with the homeless. None of this is true.

We are, on the whole, an open people, a people who realize the necessity of seeing the stranger as possibly "God returning." Hence, we are from our African roots most hospitable. Political realities, however, must be addressed. The fact of the matter is clear: The government of the United States is open to the "tired, the poor, the. . .masses yearning to breathe free" only when there is political advantage to be gained. On a governmental level, poverty and pain seem to have little to do with the resettlement of refugee populations. We Blacks know this and speak it loudly, not against persons, but for justice.

While on the one hand, we are disappointed by the apparent dishonesty of many officials, we must, as a people, open our hearts to minister to those who walk the world without homes. Our ability to see all progress in terms of spiritual good overcoming all evil determines whether or not we will transform the world. We, by our ministry to the Vietnamese, show forth again the spiritual power that Martin and Malcolm and Sojourner Truth and Harriet Tubman proved could change the world—little by little.

Being a refugee is not without pain. We Blacks know that. When out of the strength our suffering has brought we serve others, we grow stronger, and before the finish, we shall, like Christ, bestride the globe.

THERE'S LOVE IN THE AIR

Mother Teresa of Calcutta

Maybe our
children, our husband,
our wife are not hungry,
are not naked,
are not homeless.

But are you sure
there is no one there
who feels unwanted,
unloved?

Let us look
straight into our
own families.

For love begins at home.

Br. Cyprian Lamar Rowe, FMS, Ph.D., a Marist brother who is a psychotherapist at the Johns Hopkins Hospital in Baltimore, does professional clinical work with Black priests and religious. He also writes about issues that are important to their ministries and spiritual growth.

WE SHARE . . . LOVE

Family Activities

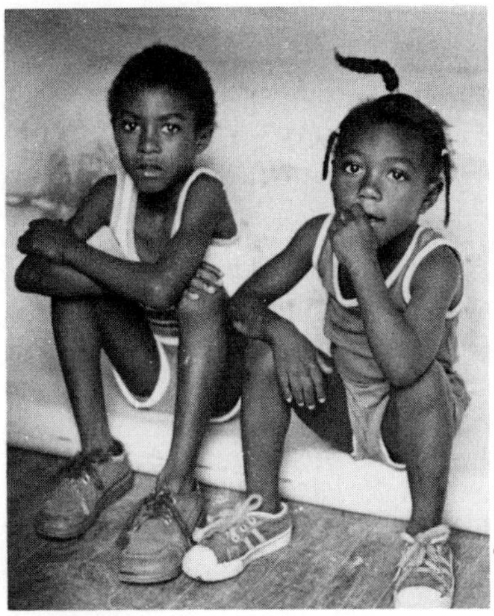

CHD/Peter Magubane

When have I felt homeless? unwanted? unloved?

Why have I felt homeless? unwanted? unloved?

How have family members shown us their love?

How do we let one another know we need a little extra TLC?

Every human being has a need and right to be loved, to have a home where he or she can put down roots and grow. The family is the first and indispensable community in which this need is met.

To Live in Christ Jesus
A pastoral letter of the bishops of the United States

Look straight into your own family. How can we ensure that no one feels unwanted or unloved?

How can we as family reach out to the homeless?

How can we as family share family love?

What people do we know who need family? babies? children? singles? clergy or religious? couples? new couples? the handicapped? the ill? the aged or aging? college students? exchange students?

In what ways can we be family for them? Sharing meals or prayer or outings? Asking them to bake a cake or to baby-sit? Becoming foster family? Adopting informally or formally?

How can we make extending family a regular part of our family prayer? planning? ministry? fun?

This, rather, is the fasting that I wish:
releasing those bound unjustly,
untying the thongs of the yoke;
Setting free the oppressed,
breaking every yoke;
Sharing your bread with the hungry,
sheltering the oppressed and the homeless;
Clothing the naked when you see them,
and not turning your back on your own.

Isaiah 58:6-7

CHD/Peter Magubane

WE SHARE . . . HISTORY

The Idea of Ancestry

ETHERIDGE KNIGHT

Courtesy of Joyce Smith

Taped to the wall of my cell are 47 pictures: 47 black faces:
my father, mother, grandmothers (1 dead), grandfathers (both
dead), brothers, sisters, uncles, aunts, cousins (1st & 2nd),
nieces, and nephews. They stare across the space at me sprawling
on my bunk. I know their dark eyes, they know mine. I know their
style, they know mine. I am all of them, they are all of me; they are
farmers, I am a thief, I am me, they are thee.

I have at one time or another been in love with my mother,
1 grandmother, 2 sisters, 2 aunts (1 went to the asylum), and
5 cousins. I am now in love with a 7 yr old niece (she sends me
letters written in large block print, and her picture is the only one
that smiles at me).

I have the same name as 1 grandfather, 3 cousins, 3 nephews,
and 1 uncle. The uncle disappeared when he was 15, just took
off and caught a freight (they say). He's discussed each year when
the family has a reunion, he causes uneasiness in the clan, he is
an empty space. My father's mother, who is 93 and who keeps the
Family Bible with everybody's birth dates (and death dates) in it,
always mentions him. There is no place in her Bible for "where-
abouts unknown."

Each Fall the graves of my grandfathers call me, the brown
hills and red gullies of mississippi send out their electric messages, galvanizing my genes. Last yr/like a salmon quitting the
cold ocean—leaping and bucking up his birthstream/I hitch
hiked my way from L.A. with 16 caps in my pocket and a monkey
on my back, and I almost kicked it with the kinfolks. I walked
barefooted in my grandmother's backyard/I smelled the old
land and the woods/I sipped cornwhisky from fruit jars with the men/
I flirted with the women/I had a ball till the caps ran out and my
habit came down. That night I looked at my grandmother and
split/my guts were screaming for junk/but I was almost con-
tented/ I had almost caught up with me.
(The next day in Memphis I cracked a croaker's crib for a fix.)

This yr there is a gray stone wall damming my stream, and when
the falling leaves stir my genes, I pace my cell or flop on my bunk
and stare at 47 black faces across the space. I am all of them,
they are all of me. I am me, they are thee, and I have no sons
to float in the space between.

Etheridge Knight, poet, describes himself as being "self-educated in various prisons and jails." He is author of *Poems From Prison* (Broadside) and *Black Voices From Prison* (Merit). His poems and short stories have appeared in *Negro Digest, Jaguar, Music Journal* and *Goliards.*

WE SHARE . . . HISTORY

Family Activities

FAMILY HISTORY

How can we as family best research and preserve our family history? What relatives and friends do we need to interview?

What family goals can we achieve through the interview process?

What places do we need to visit to get in touch with our history?

How will we record our family history? family tree? family gallery? family albums? family pictures? family stories? family sayings?

How will we enjoy sharing our family history? How will we as family grow through sharing? With whom will we share our family history?

How can we include family members who are very young, very old, far away, or alone?

Rogelio Solis/Courtesy of Mississippi Today

FAMILY RECORDS

How can we keep our family records current?

What kinds of things do we wish to record?

Family Diaries—Every family member writes in significant events. Once a month, the diary is read at family time to be sure that nothing important has been missed.

Family Tapes—Once a year, perhaps at New Year, have each family member tape a message for the family archives. Let one family member introduce each speaker. Don't forget to record the baby (if there is one). Copies of the family tape might make nice gifts for relatives who think you're special.

Family Albums—Once a year, perhaps at New Year, make sure your albums are in order and up to date. Duplicate pictures make nice family gifts.

Decide how we can use our family records to
celebrate who we are and how we have come this far by faith;
bring joy into our home;
unite with family members who are absent;
enrich our lives.

FAMILY HEROES AND HEROINES

Spend an evening sharing stories about people who have inspired you and helped you keep on keeping on—

Parents, brothers and sisters, other relatives,
priests, brothers, sisters, deacons, ministers.

Coaches, teachers, 4H or scout leaders,

Church people like Pope John XXIII, Bishop James Lyke, Mahalia Jackson, or Sister Addie Walker.

Political figures like Malcolm X or Shirley Chisholm or C.O. Chinn, Jr.

Martyrs like the young men of Uganda or Martin Luther King, Jr.

Suffering souls like Beatrice Smith.

Rogelio Solis/Courtesy of Mississippi Today

Share lessons you have learned from your heroes and heroines. Tell how you hope to follow in their footsteps or to carry the torch they pass on. Collect pictures of the people who have inspired you and make a family scrapbook or mobile or collage.

READ "LINEAGE" TOGETHER.

What does Margaret Walker Alexander tell us about her grandmothers? What did they do?

How does she feel about them? Why does she admire them?

How does she feel about herself? Why?

Share your own favorite grandparent stories with the whole family. (Don't forget adopted grandparents.)

Let each member of the family write or draw or sing or act a lineage poem that records the strength and beauty of a grandparent or a granduncle or aunt. Share these poems with the whole family.

Make a booklet of lineage poems to share with relatives who live far away.

Make family plans to visit all your older relatives to learn more about your history and heritage. Let them realize that they are your treasures.

If you don't have enough grandparents, plan to adopt some more.

Mark Grandparent's Day on your family calendar (so you won't forget to celebrate).

CHD/Barbara Baker Stephenson

Lineage

MARGARET WALKER ALEXANDER, PH.D.

My grandmothers were strong.
They followed plows and bent to toil.
They moved through fields sowing seed.
They touched earth and grain grew.
They were full of sturdiness and singing.
My grandmothers were strong.

My grandmothers are full of memories
Smelling of soap and onions and wet clay
With veins rolling roughly over quick hands
They have many clean words to say.
My grandmothers were strong.
Why am I not as they?

"Lineage," by Margaret Walker Alexander, from *For My People*, published by Yale University Press, 1942; reprinted Arno Press, 1968. Copyright © 1968 Margaret Walker Alexander. Used with permission.

Margaret Walker Alexander, Ph.D., poet and novelist, is professor emeritus of English at Jackson State University, Jackson, Mississippi, where she was also director of the Black Studies Institute. Recipient of many honors and awards, her writing includes a volume of verse, *For My People* (Yale University), and a Civil War novel, *Jubilee* (Houghton Mifflin), that has been translated into seven languages. Her poetry has been published in numerous anthologies and periodicals.

WE SHARE . . . PRAYER

Family Activities

So many times, we do not live our dreams into realities because we do not plan. The lists that follow are designed to help the family, or the community, play about prayer: What is the quality of our family prayer? How do we need to pray together? When do we need to pray together?

Look over the lists and make specific plans for family prayer that will be meaningful, that will speak in the language that your family understands, that will draw family members together in love.

Make plans for family prayer and then come back to evaluate. We said we'd pray in the morning, have we done so? Was our prayer meaningful? What can we do to improve the quality of our prayer? What can we do to teach one another to pray? Little children can teach their parents, parents can teach their children. We can reach out to grandparents, or to members of our family who live at some distance so that we become a praying family. As praying families, we share all the ways that we find prayer meaningful; then we become a praying community. When we pray in community, we then can pray in church.

When will we pray together?

- ☐ Morning Prayer
- ☐ Grace before Meals
- ☐ Grace after Meals
- ☐ Evening Prayer
- ☐ Sunday Family Mass
- ☐ Weekday Family Mass
- ☐ Prayer Meeting
- ☐ Family Retreat
- ☐ ______________________
- ☐ ______________________
- ☐ ______________________
- ☐ ______________________

How will we pray together?

- ☐ Biblical Prayer
- ☐ Visual Prayer
- ☐ Body Prayer
- ☐ Sung Prayer
- ☐ Liturgical Prayer
- ☐ Silent Prayer
- ☐ Formal Prayer
- ☐ Spontaneous Prayer
- ☐ Listening to God in Nature
- ☐ Prayer in Grief
- ☐ Prayer in Joy
- ☐ Prayer in Confusion
- ☐ Prayer in Anxiety
- ☐ Prayer in Hope
- ☐ Prayer in Faith
- ☐ ______________________
- ☐ ______________________

It is at this special moment in history when many people are coming to realize that the culture of black folk is the vehicle for the Spirit of God, and that the soulfulness, the spirituality, the spiritual dynamism always so evident in happenings among black folk is an example of what is so frequently lacking in assemblies, both within and outside the Church.

This is the kind of soul-stirring that is frequently missing from our liturgical celebrations.

This is the kind of unique gift that black folk want to bring, want to share with the Church.

Bishop Eugene A. Marino, SSJ, D.D.

"The Contribution of Black People to the Church," an address given by Bishop Eugene A. Marino, SSJ, at the 41st International Eucharistic Congress, Philadelphia, 1978.

What are our favorite forms of family prayer?

What are our favorite forms of liturgical prayer?

USCC/Nelson Brooks

How will we share responsibility for making family prayer meaningful to all?

- ☐ Writing Our Own Meal Prayers
- ☐ Creating a Family Prayer Book
- ☐ Family Rite of Reconciliation
- ☐
- ☐
- ☐
- ☐
- ☐

How can we as black folk share our unique gift of prayer with the Church?

- ☐ Thanksgiving
- ☐ Praise
- ☐ Petition
- ☐ Prayer for the Sick
- ☐ Prayer for the Dying
- ☐ Prayer for Loved Ones
- ☐ Prayer for Patience
- ☐ Prayer for Increase of Faith
- ☐ Prayer for the Suffering of the World
- ☐
- ☐
- ☐
- ☐
- ☐
- ☐
- ☐

WE SHARE . . . CELEBRATION

Family Activities

Courtesy of the John Reese Family

By celebrating who we are and what we hope to become, we share our faith; we share our values; we share our love. Most of us don't celebrate enough.

Have the family come together and do some planning, make some new decisions: What will we celebrate? Will we celebrate birthdays, namings, name days? How will we celebrate? The community, the family of families, can then come together and make some decisions about the celebration that shares our joys, our griefs, and our lives together.

Later, come back to evaluate. We decided to celebrate. Was the celebration meaningful to us? Was it significant? Did it have any lasting results in our lives? Do we want to do it again?

How can we as black Catholics celebrate God's love from our experience?

____

____

____

How can we share our gift of blackness with the Church?

____

____

____

What Will We Celebrate?

- ☐ Birthdays
- ☐ Namings
- ☐ Name Days
- ☐ Weddings
- ☐ Funerals
- ☐ Anniversaries
- ☐ Graduations
- ☐ Reunions
- ☐ Harvest Festival
- ☐ Kwanza
- ☐ Senior Citizens Night
- ☐ Young Peoples Day
- ☐ Black History Month
- ☐ Homecoming
- ☐ ____________________
- ☐ ____________________
- ☐ Mother's Day
- ☐ Father's Day
- ☐ Grandparent's Day
- ☐ Family Joys
- ☐ Family Griefs
- ☐ Adoptions formal/informal
- ☐ New Friends
- ☐ ____________________
- ☐ Favorite Teacher Night
- ☐ Halloween
- ☐ Veterans Day
- ☐ Valentine's Day
- ☐ First Day of Spring
- ☐ Memorial Day
- ☐ Labor Day
- ☐ ____________________
- ☐ A Good Report Card
- ☐ Grandma's Visit
- ☐ Losing a Baby Tooth
- ☐ ____________________
- ☐ ____________________
- ☐ ____________________
- ☐ ____________________
- ☐ ____________________
- ☐ Sojourner Truth
- ☐ Malcolm X

☐ Martin Luther King, Jr.
☐ ______________________
☐ ______________________
☐ ______________________
☐ ______________________
☐ ______________________
☐ Baptism
☐ Eucharist
☐ Reconciliation
☐ Sacramental Anniversaries
☐ ______________________
☐ ______________________
☐ ______________________
☐ ______________________
☐ Advent
☐ Christmas
☐ Epiphany
☐ Lent
☐ Easter
☐ Eves & Vigils of Special Feasts
☐ New Year's
☐ ______________________
☐ Benedict the Moor—April 3
☐ Charles Lwanga & Companions—June 3
☐ Monica—August 27
☐ Augustine—August 28
☐ Martin de Porres—November 3
☐ ______________________
☐ ______________________
☐ ______________________

How Will We Celebrate?

☐ Gifts
☐ Homemade Gifts
☐ Recycled Gifts
☐ Gifts of Time
☐ Gifts of Service
☐ Cards
☐ Homemade Cards
☐ Passing on a Family Heirloom
☐ Baby Books
☐ Scrapbooks
☐ Collages
☐ Home Tapes and Movies
☐ Bronzed Baby Booties
☐ Home Decorations
☐ Flowers
☐ Retelling Family Stories
☐ Breakfasts in Bed
☐ Brunches
☐ Pancake Suppers
☐ Hugging Family Members
☐ Saying "I Love You"
☐ Sharing a Tootsie Roll
☐ Kissing Grandpa Goodnight
☐ ______________________
☐ Parties
☐ Picnics
☐ Block Parties
☐ Potlucks
☐ P.T.A. Programs
☐ Skits and Pantomimes
☐ Dances
☐ Songfests
☐ Phone Calls
☐ Visits
☐ Letters
☐ Newspaper Clippings
☐ Graffiti
☐ ______________________
☐ Heritage Tours
☐ Museum Trips
☐ Open House
☐ Free Baby Sitting
☐ Caroling for Shut-ins
☐ Sharing a Poverty Meal & Giving Money Saved to the Poor
☐ ______________________
☐ ______________________
☐ Banners
☐ Incense
☐ Paintings, Drawings, and Statues
☐ Proclamation of the Word
☐ Preaching
☐ Witnessing, Testifying
☐ Shouting
☐ *Soulfull Worship*[1]
☐ Gospel Choirs
☐ Classical Choirs
☐ Liturgical Song

Rogelio Solis/Courtesy of Mississippi Today

- ☐ Liturgical Dance
- ☐ Liturgical Drama
- ☐ ______________________
- ☐ ______________________
- ☐ ______________________
- ☐ Family Liturgy
- ☐ Neighborhood Liturgy (four or five families)
- ☐ Inter-Parish Liturgy
- ☐ The Passover (Seder) Meal
- ☐ ______________________
- ☐ ______________________
- ☐ ______________________
- ☐ ______________________

Some of the celebrating we do ritualizes who we are. There are thousands of ways we celebrate. We have teen-agers. We have young people who say they don't have anything to do. We have old people who are lonely. How can we celebrate our faith, our values, our love?

Think of what you want to do in order to celebrate. What do you as community want to do to celebrate the family bonds that exist in community? the family bonds that exist in Church?

Make plans, act, and then evaluate. We said we'd celebrate. Did we really do so?

NOTE

1. Clarence Jos. Rivers, Jr., "Ingredients of Effective Worship," in *The Spirit in Worship*, a two-volume set on worship, *I Soulfull Worship; II The Spirit in Worship*. (Cincinnati: Stimuli, Inc., 1978).

Courtesy of the John Reese Family

WE SHARE . . . CELEBRATION

A Paraliturgical Celebration of the Nguzo Saba, the Black Value System

FR. FERNAND J. CHERI III AND TONI BALOT

Theme: By living the values of our ancestors we participate in the creation of a New People.

INTRODUCTORY RITE

Opening Hymn: PLENTY GOOD ROOM

Plenty good room, plenty good room,
Plenty good room in my Father's kingdom;
Plenty good room, plenty good room,
So choose your seat and sit down.

I would not be a liar and I'll tell you the reason why
'Cause if my Lord should call my name
I wouldn't be ready to die.
So I'm glad that there's . . . .

Plenty good room. . . .

I would not be a back slider and I'll tell you the reason why
'Cause if my Lord were calling me
I wouldn't be ready to die.
So I'm glad that there's . . . .

Plenty good room. . . .

I'm so high and I'm so low,
Oh, my Lord.
I've been through trials big enough
Knowing he's my Lord.
So I bear witness to . . . .

Plenty good room . . . .

My Lord said there's room enough,
Oh, my Lord.
There's room for you and even room for me,
Oh, my Lord.
So I'm glad that there's . . . .

Plenty good room . . . .

Greeting

Presider: To you the Black Church ________________________(parish name)
"The challenge of Blackness is the challenge
of living today in tomorrow's truth.
It is the challenge of internalizing
and carrying around with us the reborn Black Community."[1]
This is what we have gathered to work toward tonight,
And this is what we now come to pray to
our Almighty God about. . . .

Fr. Fernand J. Cheri III is administrator of St. Joseph the Worker Church in Marrero, Louisiana. He serves on the board of directors of the National Black Catholic Clergy Caucus and was cochairperson of the 1984 joint conference of that organization, the National Black Sisters' Conference and the National Black Catholic Seminarians' Association. When he collaborated in writing *A Paraliturgical Celebration of the Nguzo Saba, the Black Value System,* he was on the parish team of Sacred Heart of Jesus Church in New Orleans.

Toni Balot is a social worker in the New Orleans public schools. She is a resource person for children's liturgies at St. Agnes Church, Jefferson, Mississippi. When she collaborated in the writing of *A Paraliturgical Celebration of the Nguzo Saba, the Black Value System,* she was on the pastoral team of Sacred Heart of Jesus Church in New Orleans.

and so we begin in the spirit of holiness and
of true Catholicity
(Sing or recite):
In the name of the Father,
In the name of the Son,
In the name of the Spirit,
the blest three in one.[2]

All: Amen.

PRAYER

Presider: Let us pray: (Pause.)
O God, our Father,
bless us tonight as we gather here to praise you.
Bless these symbols which we have here before us. . . .
Symbols of our African tradition which were used by our ancestors.
Bless these candles which represent the values
lived by our ancestors,
and which we now wish to make part of our lives.
Give us understanding and wisdom, Father,
that we may know how you wish us to free each other,
and give us the courage and strength to do this.
All this we ask in the name of Jesus, our Brother and Liberator.

All: Amen.

LITURGY OF THE WORD

First Reading

Presider: God reveals himself to us in many ways.
His first revelation to us tonight will be through
song and light and explanations about our values.

Cantor: Gimme dat ol' time religion,
Gimme dat ol' time religion, It's good enough for me.

All: Gimme dat ol' time religion
Gimme dat ol' time religion
Gimme dat ol' time religion, It's good enough for me.

First Reader: UMOJA—Unity: (Pause while the candle is lighted.)
To strive for and maintain unity in the family, community,
nation, and race.

Cantor: Gimme dat ol' time religion. . . .

Second Reader: KUJICHAGULIA—Self-determination: (Pause, light candle.)
To define ourselves, create for ourselves, and speak for ourselves.

Cantor: Gimme dat ol' time religion. . . .

Third Reader: UJIMA—Collective Work and Responsibility: (Pause.)
To build and maintain our community together and make our
brothers' and sisters' problems our problems and to solve
them together.

Cantor: Gimme dat ol' time religion. . . .

Fourth Reader: UJAMAA—Cooperative Economics: (Pause.)
To build and maintain our own stores, shops, and other
businesses, and to profit from them together.

Cantor: Gimme dat ol' time religion. . . .

Fifth Reader: NIA—Purpose: (Pause.)
To make as our collective vocation the building and developing of our community in order to restore our people to their traditional greatness.

Cantor: Gimme dat ol' time religion. . . .

Sixth Reader: KUUMBA—Creativity: (Pause.)
To do always as much as we can in the way we can in order to leave our community more beautiful and beneficial than when we inherited it.

Cantor: Gimme dat ol' time religion. . . .

Seventh Reader: IMANI—Faith: (Pause.)
To believe with all our heart in our parents, our teachers, our leaders, our people, and our God, and in the righteousness and victory of our struggle[3]

Cantor: Gimme dat ol' time religion. . . .

Presider: (After a suitable pause.)
In the Book of Revelation, God promises us a new heaven and a new earth where he himself will dwell with us in freedom.

Lector: "Then I saw a new earth and a new sky, for the present earth and sky had disappeared. And I . . . saw the Holy City, the new Jerusalem, coming down from God out of heaven. It was a glorious sight, beautiful as a bride at her wedding. I heard a loud shout from the throne saying, 'Look, the home of God is now among men, and he will live with them and they will be his people; yes, God himself will be among them. He will wipe away all tears from their eyes, and there shall be no more death, nor sorrow, nor crying, nor pain. All of that has gone forever.'

"And the one sitting on the throne said, 'See, I am making all things new! . . . I will give to the thirsty the springs of the Water of Life—as a gift! Everyone who conquers will inherit all these blessings, and I will be his God and he will be my Son.' . . . Then he who is seated upon the throne said, 'See, I am making all things new! Come! . . . Let the thirsty come, and let everyone who wishes take the water of life as a gift.' "[4]

Homily

Presider: AIM: To enable our people to realize that by going back to our old tradition, and living the values of our ancestors, we participate in the creation of the new earth, the new people, who it is our privilege and responsibility to reveal to today's world.

CLOSING PRAYER

Presider: O Christ, our Brother, our Messiah in Blackness, help us to realize the Afro-American past that we are heirs to; a tradition and a heritage of Black freedom fighters who made it possible for us to stand here in prayer today and search for new ways to overcome this racism that eats into the conscience of this nation.

Help us to be an inspiration to each other—just as we ourselves have been inspired by men and women like Malcolm and Martin, Angela Davis and Coretta.
Help us to be true to the tradition of those Blacks who dared to take a stand—and those who suffer today because of the stand they do take.[5]

We ask this through the power of your Spirit who lives with you and the Father forever and ever.

All: Amen.

CLOSING SONG

Cantor: LIFT EVERY VOICE AND SING

CHD/Peter Magubane

LIFT EV'RY VOICE AND SING

Arranged by Marcel Frank

J. ROSAMOND JOHNSON

G
A Little Slower
G6
sea. Sing a song full of the faith that the dark past has
sighed? We have come o - ver a way that with tears has been
pray. Lest our feet stray from the pla - ces, our God, where we
G
G(+5)
G G♯dim
taught us; Sing a song full of the hope that the pre - sent has brought
wa - tered; We have come, tread - ing our path thro' the blood of the slaugh -
met Thee, Lest our hearts, drunk with the wine of the world, we for - get
Original time
D7
G B7 E
Am B7 Em Eb
us; Fac - ing the ris - ing sun of our new day be - gun, Let us march
tered, Out from the gloom - y past. Till now we stand at last Where the white
Thee; Shad - owed be - neath Thy hand, May we for - ev - er stand True to our
1.2.
3.
G C6 D C/D G Am7 G D G Am7 G
on till vic - to - ry is won. 2. Ston - y the
gleam of our bright star is cast. 3. God of our
God, True to our na - tive land.

In the words of the old spiritual, our people left us as heritage a no-fail design for building family, community, Church:

WALK TOGETHER CHILDREN

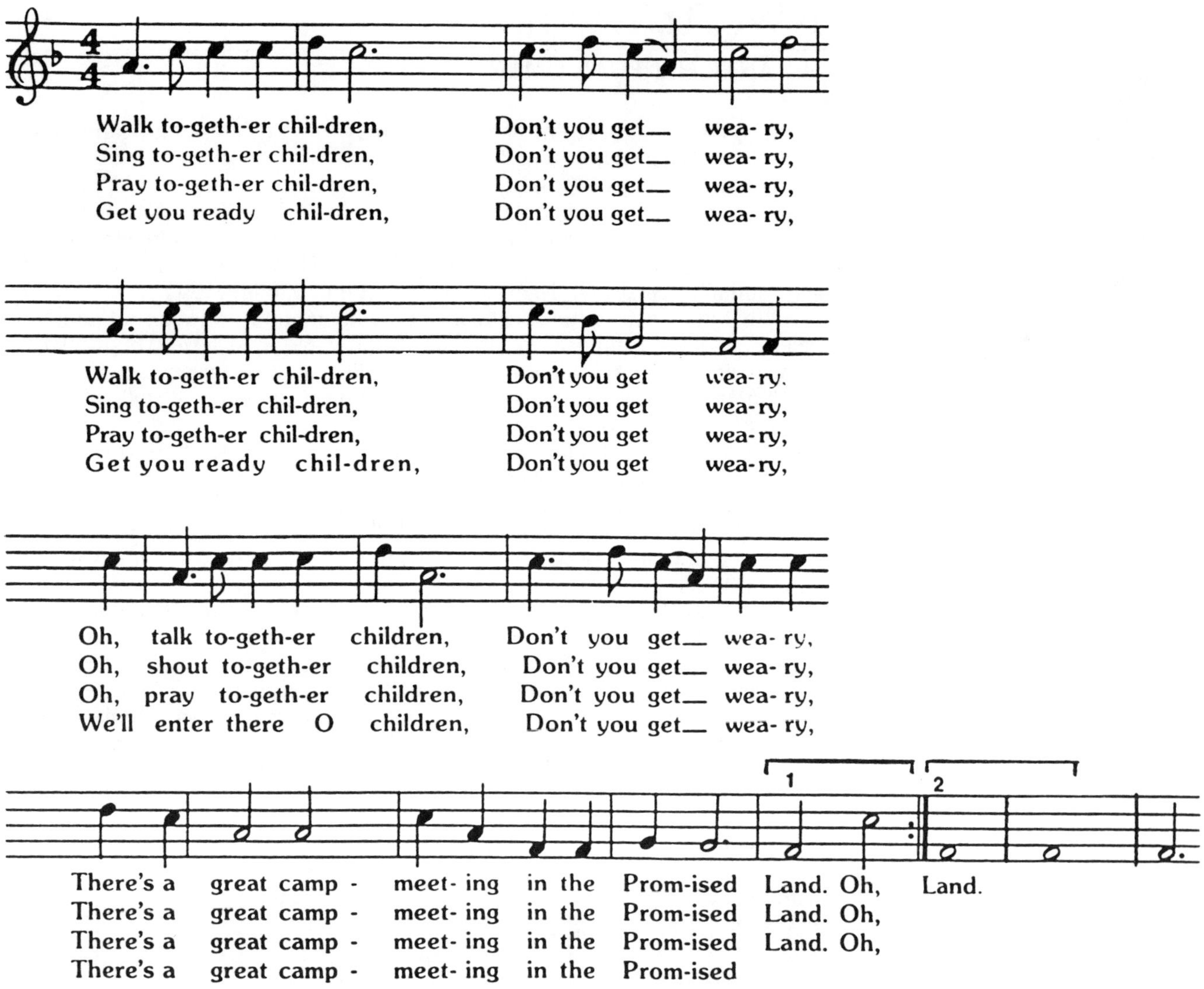
Walk to-geth-er chil-dren, Don't you get wea- ry,
Sing to-geth-er chil-dren, Don't you get wea- ry,
Pray to-geth-er chil-dren, Don't you get wea- ry,
Get you ready chil-dren, Don't you get wea- ry,
Walk to-geth-er chil-dren, Don't you get wea-ry,
Sing to-geth-er chil-dren, Don't you get wea-ry,
Pray to-geth-er chil-dren, Don't you get wea-ry,
Get you ready chil-dren, Don't you get wea-ry,
Oh, talk to-geth-er children, Don't you get wea- ry,
Oh, shout to-geth-er children, Don't you get wea- ry,
Oh, pray to-geth-er children, Don't you get wea- ry,
We'll enter there O children, Don't you get wea- ry,
1
2
There's a great camp - meet- ing in the Prom-ised Land. Oh, Land.
There's a great camp - meet- ing in the Prom-ised Land. Oh,
There's a great camp - meet- ing in the Prom-ised Land. Oh,
There's a great camp - meet- ing in the Prom-ised

NOTES

1. Lerone Bennett, Jr., *The Challenge of Blackness* (Chicago: Johnson Publishing Co., 1972), 17.
2. Use of the tune from "Black Thankfulness," by Clarence Jos. Rivers, Jr., is suggested here. (Cincinnati: Stimuli, Inc.).
3. Definitions of the Seven Black Values are taken from "The Nguzo Saba," by Maulana Ron Karenga. In *Freeing the Spirit* 1, August 1971. (Washington, D.C.: National Office for Black Catholics).
4. Revelations 21: 1–5; 22:17
5. "Soulful Samplings of Prayer," in *Freeing the Spirit* 1, August 1971. (Washington, D.C.: National Office for Black Catholics), 39.

***A Paraliturgical Celebration of the Nguzo Saba,* developed by Rev. Fernand J. Cheri III, and Ms. Toni Balot for use in Black Values Workshop for Black Catholic Families, Sacred Heart of Jesus Parish, New Orleans, Louisiana. Used with permission.**

WE SHARE . . . CELEBRATION

Afro-Alternative to Christmas Kwanza

Ms. ANNE HENEHAN OMAN

When you get tired of saying "Merry Christmas," try saying "Habari gani?" It's Swahili for "What's happening?"

On the first day of Kwanza, December 26, the correct answer to "What's happening?" is Umoja, which means "unity." Each of the seven days of the celebration stresses a particular principle, such as Kujichagulia (self-determination), Ujima (collective work and responsibility), Ujamaa (cooperative economics), Kuumba (creativity), Nia (purpose), and Imani (faith). . . .

What the creche is to Christmas and the menorah is to Hanukkah, the mkeka, kinara, mushumaa, zawadi, and muhindi are to Kwanza. The mkeka, a straw mat, represents tradition as the foundation on which everything rests. The kinara, a seven-place candleholder, symbolizes the original stalk from which black people originated. The mushumaa, or candles, stand for the seven principles. The corn (muhindi) represents the children of the house. The bowl of zawadi, or gifts, represents the fruits of labor.

The gifts should be small handmade items, or things that have a special meaning that will help the person through the next year. The gifts, which can't be opened until the last day of the celebration, are placed on the mat with the other symbols.

Each day the family gets together and lights the candle for that day and talks about the principle for the day. Then they pour a libation—usually gin or vodka—into the ground to honor their ancestors. In some houses it is poured into a basket filled with earth.

The last day, January 1, features a feast, or karamu. In some homes, the feast features black-eyed peas and rice, which coincides with the Afro-American and Southern tradition offering these foods on New Year's Day.

A BOWL FOR THE ZAWADI (GIFTS)

You will need:
- A bowl
- Lard
- Newspapers
- Flour (or liquid white glue)
- Water
- Paint
- Shellac (optional)

Directions:
- Tear the newspaper into strips.
- Thoroughly grease the outside of the bowl with lard.
- Combine flour and water (or glue and water). The consistency should be that of a thick pancake mix.
- Moisten the strips of paper with the paste and cover the bowl with several layers.
- Let the paper dry, and then carefully remove it from the bowl.
- Trim the edge with scissors.
- Paint it, and when the paint is dry apply a thin coat of shellac or liquid white glue.

You are now ready to fill the bowl you've made with fruits, nuts, and at least one ear of corn.

Anne Henehan Oman is a free-lance writer who contributes frequently to the *Washington Post* and National Geographic Society publications.

THE MKEKA (STRAW HAT)

You will need:

- Newspapers
- A stapler
- Paint
- Shellac

Directions:

- Fold the newspaper, a sheet at a time, into strips about 2" wide.
- Make a U-shaped frame by stapling three of these strips together, interlocking their ends for the corners. The open sides of the strips should be on the inside of the U.
- Fill in the base of the U with strips, stapling them in place.
- Weave in the cross-strips, stapling them into the slots in the side of the U.
- Close the open side of the U, stapling the ends of the vertical strips into slot and interlocking the corners as above.
- Paint the mat and, when the paint is dry, apply a thin coat of shellac.

"Afro-Alternative to Christmas—Kwanza," by Anne H. Oman, originally published in *The Washington Post* (December 23, 1977). Reprinted with permission.

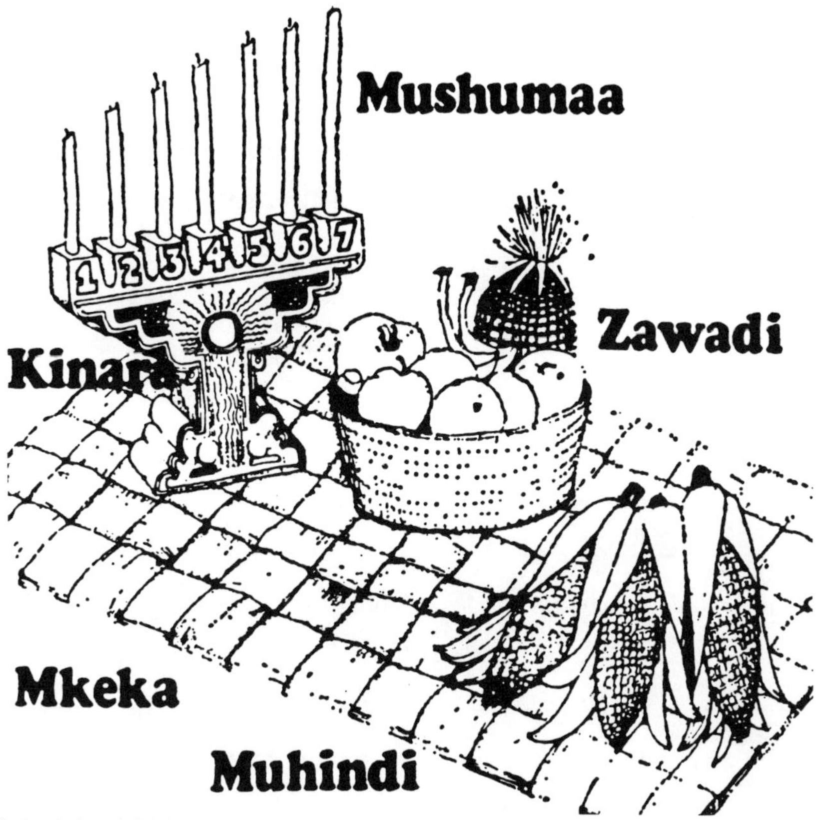

Illustration from the Anacostia Neighborhood Museum's Kwanza Kit

WE SHARE . . . DREAMS

Family Activities

What are our dreams as individuals?

What are our dreams as a family?

If each of us had three wishes, what would they be?

If we as a family had three wishes, what would they be?

What happens when dreams die?

How can we encourage one another to "hold fast to dreams"?

What does dreaming together mean?

What does dreaming together demand?

DREAMS
Langston Hughes

Hold fast to dreams
For if dreams die
Life is a broken-winged bird
That cannot fly.

Hold fast to dreams
For when dreams go
Life is a barren field
Frozen with snow.

How can we as family begin to make individual and family dreams *reality*?

CHD/Peter Magubane

When we dream alone
it is only a dream,
But
when we
dream
together
it is
the
beginning
of
REALITY

Brazilian Proverb

WE SHARE . . . GOALS

Black Competence

ANDREW BILLINGSLEY, Ph.D.

One of the major goals and achievements among our Black families is developing a sense of competence on the part of individual family members, especially the young. Families must instill in the young a sense of mastery, a quest for achievement, a set of interpersonal skills, and the desire to acquire technical skills in order to function in the world. The fact that most Black children do, in fact, acquire these basic competencies within the framework of their families is a tribute to the effectiveness of Black family life. The fact that many do not achieve these qualities is a measure of the odds against which the families must struggle. The goal of Black family life, then, is to produce competent individuals, people able to be, to know, to do, and above all, to think. These are the requisites of survival.

Sr. Angela Williams

Andrew Billingsley, Ph.D., is professor of sociology and Afro-American studies at the University of Maryland. A former president of Morgan State University in Baltimore, he was visiting scholar and professor of social welfare at the Institute for the Study of Social Change of the University of California, Berkeley. His extensive writing includes the influential *Black Families in White America* (Prentice-Hall), *Children of the Storm* (Harcourt, Brace) and *Black Families and the Struggle for Survival* (Friendship Press). Articles by Dr. Billingsley have appeared in many professional publications, and he has testified on behalf of families before congressional committees.

WE SHARE . . . GOALS

A Coping Strategy for Survival of the Black Catholic Family

EDWIN J. NICHOLS, PH.D.

USCC/Nelson Brooks

The higher your educational level, the higher your entry point into the economic system. Racism, however, limits your advancement within the system once you have entered it.

EDUCATIONAL ISSUES: THE POLITICALIZATION OF YOUR CHILDREN

To create a learning environment, the parents must demonstrate that they place a high value on learning. Let your children see you reading a book, then discuss it with them. Be near them while they are doing their homework and studying; it means you are concerned.

Limit unsupervised TV watching (garbage in, garbage out). Watch TV together using it as a forum to discuss moral values, social issues, logic systems used to define you, such as advertising with hidden agenda. Listen to your child's answers. Cut the TV off, read reference materials, facts and figures—Was what was said on the TV exist in fact?

A politicalized child will not become a victim of the "truths" of the ideology presented in the media.

RELIGIOUS ISSUES: PRAYER CHANGES THINGS

Prayer changes the individual so that he can cope with that which is without the self. Do not embarrass your children with great overt shows of compulsory family prayer hour. It is better to teach them the power of individual private devotion . . . . This skill they can take with them away from home. Your personal example leaves its imprint more than words. . . . As a middle-aged man, I have never seen my father put a spoonful of food to his mouth without saying a grace, silently much of the time, so not to intrude upon the privacy of others.

SOCIAL ISSUES: EVERYBODY ELSE IS DOING IT, WHY CAN'T I?

When social issues such as dating, smoking, drinking, pot, drugs, sex, VD, teen-age pregnancy, etc., come up—discuss them openly, express your moral and social values on the topic.

All the other kids are doing it; that means that you are letting others define you. Politicalization shows one of the pitfalls of that reasoning.

Smoking, drinking, pills; ask what are the hidden agenda, who is making the money, how much money is being made. Look in your reference book and see how much tax is collected on alcohol and tobacco by the United States Treasury. Now it is easy to understand why the government will say that tobacco is bad for your health, but does not stop farm subsidy to tobacco farmers. If pot could be taxed today, it would have been legal yesterday.

AS PARENTS IN BLACK CATHOLIC FAMILIES, OUR GOALS ARE TO

- Program our children to define themselves.
- Think critically, with a moral referent, about daily issues they face.
- Make sound judgments about what decisions cost them, a personalized cost/effectiveness ratio accounting system.

"A Coping Strategy for Survival of the Black Catholic Family," Edwin J. Nichols, Ph.D., from *The Black Catholic Family: A Change Agent for the Church*, Paper for the Conference on the Apostolate of the Church in the Black Community (Hendersonville, N.C., 1979).

Edwin J. Nichols, Ph.D., chief of the Staff College of the National Institute of Mental Health, Rockville, Maryland, was a visiting professor at the University of Ibadan, Nigeria, where he directed the Child's Clinic. Educated in Canada and Germany, he received his Doctor of Philosophy cum laude from Leopol-Franz Universitat, Austria. He maintains a private clinical and industrial psychological practice.

WE SHARE . . . GOALS

Family Activities

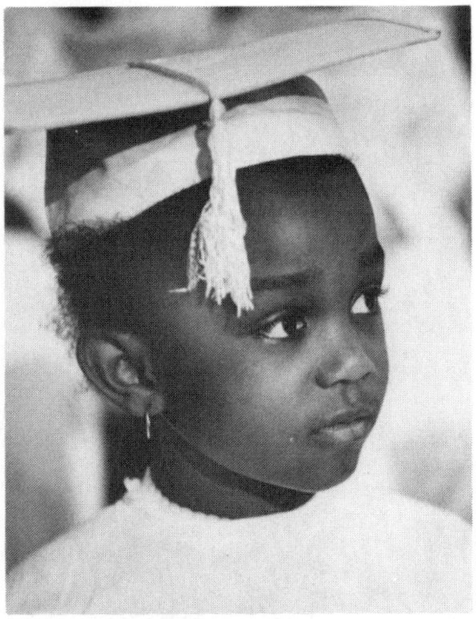

USCC/Nelson Brooks

What are our goals as a family?

What are our goals as a black family?

What are our goals as a black Catholic family?

How can we help one another to develop a sense of competence?

a sense of mastery?

a quest for achievement?

interpersonal and technical skills?

Our family goals are those accepted and owned by all of us together. In love and prayer, how can we plan and work to achieve these goals?

Rogelio Solis/Courtesy of Mississippi Today

WE SHARE . . . PLANS

Family Activities

Decide how we as *family* will

proclaim the Word to one another sharing Scripture, religious reading, story, and song.

worship the Lord together at home, in our parish, in our neighborhood, in our community.

witness to the Good News of God's Love by serving, sharing food with the hungry, sight with the blind, mobility with the crippled, freedom with the powerless and oppressed.

FAMILY MEETINGS

How often should we conduct family meetings?

When should we have them?

Where should we have them?

Who will set the agenda?

How will we be sure that everybody listens to each family member's needs and wants?

How will we be sure that we all are able to express clearly our ideas and feelings and needs and wants?

How will we be sure to look for the many possible solutions to family problems?

How will we be sure that each family member participates as fully as possible in family decision making?

Rogelio Solis/Courtesy of Mississippi Today

What can we do to make our good life together better?

How can we as parents plan together to achieve our goals?

How can we inspire and empower our children to plan with us as a family?

How can we plan effectively so that our family actions are focused toward accomplishment of family goals?

FAMILY TIME

We become Family, Community, Church by
sharing Life.

We need time to share,
to remember and dream,
to pray, play, plan,
serve, celebrate,
love and grow
AS FAMILY.

It's too important to leave to chance.

Decide as family on regular times when you will be together as family, to get to know each other better, to achieve family goals in family ways, to share life.

- Sunday mornings for Mass and brunch and Sunday afternoons till three o'clock for family fun and sharing
- Thursday evenings from five o'clock until bedtime
- Saturday mornings for family prayers and planning, with Thursday eight o'clock for family fun
- One whole weekend a month for all of the above

FAMILY CALENDARS

Make and maintain a calendar showing dates you wish to commemorate each year: birthdays, deaths, anniversaries, holidays, family holy days. Copies of this calendar might make nice gifts for family members who live far away.

Make and maintain a calendar showing family events for the coming months: John's gospel choir concert, Sarah's graduation from law school, the dog's appointment with the vet, an expected visit from Aunt Clara, a family trip, a home liturgy with the Bradley family, a Little League game.

Hang both calendars together in a family room. Appoint one family member to give calendar assistance to each member who does not read or write.

CHD/Peter Magubane

WE SHARE . . . WORK

Family Activities

How can we share the responsibility of family work?

____

____

____

What do we hope to gain by working together?

____

____

____

How can we make family work enjoyable?

____

____

____

How can we grow as family by working together?

____

____

____

How does our family work help to further our family goals?

____

____

____

CHD/Barbara Baker Stephenson

Our family work will include

- ☐ Sharing Routine Household Tasks
- ☐ Sharing Yard Maintenance
- ☐ Helping with Meals and Kitchen Cleanup
- ☐ Washing and Polishing the Car
- ☐ Gardening Together
- ☐ Sharing Spring Cleanup
- ☐ Baby Sitting
- ☐ Running Errands
- ☐ Baby Sitting Free for a Needy Family
- ☐ Running Errands and Doing Chores for a Shut-in
- ☐ ____________________
- ☐ ____________________
- ☐ ____________________
- ☐ ____________________
- ☐ ____________________
- ☐ ____________________

WE SHARE . . . FUN

Family Activities

FUN IS SHARING. SHARING IS FUN.

FAMILY MEALS
picnics, barbecues, fish fries, trips to McDonald's

FAMILY TRIPS
in cars, on bikes or skates or skateboards, or on foot
to a park, to a museum, on a nature walk
to visit friends or relatives or share joy at the hospital or nursing home
to church supper socials, singings, bingos, bazaars

FAMILY GAMES
Playing cards, tennis, checkers, chess, backgammon
Doing puzzles, jigsaw, crossword, word games
Riding horses or roller coasters or rolling old tires

FAMILY DANCING
You teach me. Then I'll teach you.

FAMILY SINGING
Sharing favorite songs, dances, tapes, records,
spirituals, gospel, classical, jazz, blues, country, old songs, new songs

FAMILY HOBBIES
gardening, sewing, cooking, raising fish, hunting birds, collecting, camping, drawing

Learning a craft
How many fun and family things can we do with an old tire, orange crate, oatmeal box, ball of yarn?

Reading stories
Telling stories

Watching good family TV
with popcorn or snacks

CHD/Peter Magubane

WE SHARE . . . MINISTRY

Training Religious Leaders for a New Black Generation

TOINETTE M. EUGENE, PH.D.

Three areas are critical to the understanding and realization of what it means to be black and Catholic in America . . . . They would form the warp and woof for any patterns for religious education programs in black parishes or black community involvement programs: (1) knowledge of contemporary black theology; (2) use of a relevant black catechesis; (3) celebration of this knowledge and catechesis in authentic black liturgy.

A problem of religious education of black people within the Catholic Church, particularly a problem with black youth, is this: There is neither reverence nor room for the very signs and symbols of black liberation within the larger society and structure of the Church. Consequently, the Church is decaying in the black community, either from direct anarchy or, more pitifully still, from the slow atrophy of no more converts, no more religious vocations, no more youth, no more collections, no more anything. Black identity and advocacy must be introduced if the spirit of the Church is to retain, or regain, vibrancy and viability in the black community.

A black catechesis is the catechetics of survival. At this moment in time, the black community is seeking to express its faith in language and in actions that fit into its contemporary mood and experience. Sources for such faith-filled movements are obvious and available both within the Catholic tradition and within the broader Christian tradition. We must discover and develop simple concepts and thematics in a "catechism of communal participation," in the need to develop indigenous leadership, and in the propagation of authentic Afro-American identity and values.

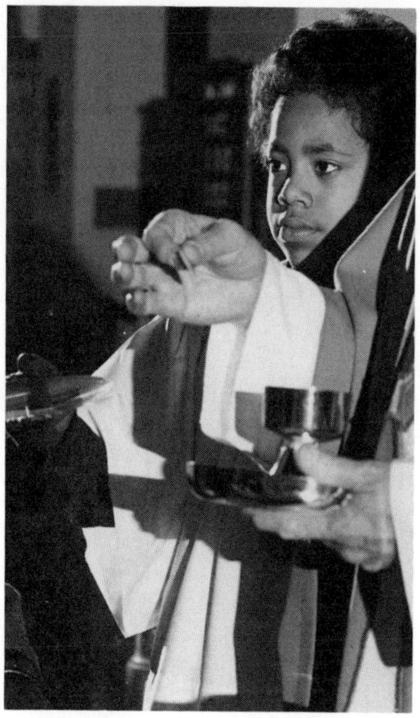
USCC/Lou Niznik

The concept of nation-building time—the gathering of black people for a communal purpose—is not foreign to Old or New Testament revelation in which people are vivified by the Spirit. The identity experience of answering "I am" to the question of "What's happening?" is infinitely important in gathering the self-affirmation present in the rest of God's people; such an identity experience is of vital import to the deflated egos of many black adolescents. "Who are you?" "What do you want?" and "What do you desire?" are questions that invite decision making. More, they invite a *yes* to freedom and a *no* to civic and ecclesial oppression. This process is an essential element for a black catechesis that seeks to elevate the age-old legacy of the universal black experience: suffering and humiliation. Although the black life experience for poor, urban youth may be different in style from that of an upward bound, middle-class black counterpart, the elements of self-esteem, pride in black heritage, and respect for the oppressed experience of all black people are essentials that should not be omitted from the religious training of either.

The catechism of participation encourages poetry, role-playing, drama, and as much articulation as possible. Passivity will not do in nation building or in the new black generation. Black abilities in dance, of spontaneous expression as part of communal prayer, can become incorporated into sessions of learning how to reach the universal Lord of Liberation through a black experience. It is this kind of prayer, this kind of worship and catechesis, that offers hope for the whole Catholic Church in America.

Communicative involvement and expression, self-determining experiences centered in Jesus the Liberator, are in. God as Father and the family of God are not difficult concepts to teach a single-parent child who is himself a part of an extended family. God can become for him the giver of dignity, of identity, of manhood. Jesus can become a "real down brother," the one who knew what time it was, for young, gifted, and black children. The Holy Spirit can be taught

Toinette M. Eugene, Ph.D., serves as assistant professor of education, society, and Black church studies at Colgate Rochester Divinity School in Rochester, New York. Dr. Eugene has published a variety of articles and essays concerning Black Catholicism and religious education.

in terms of the Soul of God, the Gift of Power to the people—right on! Black values in sign (i.e., the soul handshake); black images of the Madonna and the Messiah; black messages like "Dig your black self!", "Salaam" instead of "Shalom" on banners; and black soul songs replacing white meditation music are available to black catechetics as relevant media and message materials.

"Training Religious Leaders for a New Black Generation," Toinette M. Eugene, originally published in the *Catechist,* Vol. 6 No. 2 (October 1972). Copyright © 1972 *Catechist,* Peter Li, Inc., Dayton, Ohio 45439. Reprinted with permission.

Rogelio Solis/Courtesy of Mississippi Today

WE SHARE . . . MINISTRY

Black Religious Vocations

FR. GILES A. CONWILL, PH.D. CANDIDATE

If you make your culture *the culture,* you won't go looking for vocations among members of other cultures. If Christ's message is associated with only one culture, how can you expect Christ-loving, energetically aggressive, intelligent members of ethnic groups to divest themselves of their culture and their cultural heritage to become "white washed" by the system, and then be effective ministers to their own people? Of course, vocations won't be harvested among them . . . .

There are still many missionaries working in the Black communities of the U.S. Anyone who is not Black who ministers to or in the Black community is a "missionary." These dedicated persons deserve credit and praise for their years of sacrifice and for their contributions; however, they must always remember that they are missionaries. Proper missiology requires that one becomes very acquainted with the culture and language of the people served. Proper missiology requires that one raise up native clergy and religious, taking the posture that one will, someday, leave the direction of the Church in "native" hands. It is not that we ask that these dedicated missionaries leave our communities. Definitely not. We simply ask that they work with such diligence in developing a firm religious foundation, and in raising up a native clergy and lay leadership *as if* they were going to leave. That mental attitude would provide more motivation in the process of vocational promotion and Black leadership development . . . .

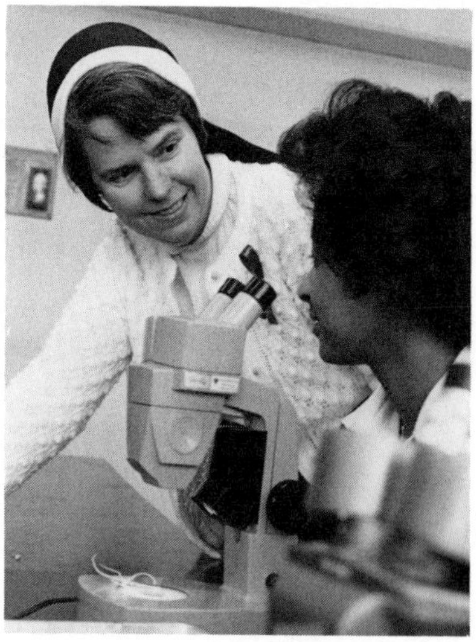

USCC/Lou Niznik

Blacks (through their local offices of Black Catholic Ministry) and concerned non-Blacks should make significant input into any agency that sets policy and standards in formation centers. Black students should not be afraid to confront their faculties and state: "If you cannot have curricula and professors that reflect me, then you aren't preparing me for ministry! You are giving me a fraudulent theological education!". . .

I would encourage seminaries and convents to send their professors and faculty personnel to National Office for Black Catholics (NOBC) Pastoral Institutes, The Institute for Black Catholic Studies at Xavier University in New Orleans, NOBC Culture and Worship Workshops. They could make sure that Black Catholic resources such as the published proceedings of the Black Catholic Theological Symposium, produced by the National Black Catholic Clergy Caucus, and *Tell It Like It Is: Religious Education from a Black Perspective,* produced by the National Black Sisters' Conference, are included. They should stock their libraries with books dealing with Black culture and Black religion and Black history. They should also make extensive use of the faculty and resources of the Black Studies departments of nearby universities.

Individual parishes or parish clusters should be encouraged to (1) implement their parish vocational committees to place vocation ads and news in local newspapers, both secular and religious; (2) develop programs to stimulate local creativity in vocation education; (3) encourage response to church vocations; (4) produce their own posters for vocations; (5) produce their own inexpensive slide presentations, using pictures of local persons engaged in ministry and asking Black religious living in nearby parishes, cities, or states to take part; (6) share these programs with diocesan and religious vocation directors, Newman chaplains, university campus ministers, and career counselors at local high schools.

Liturgical adaptation greatly affects both evangelization and, subsequently, vocation attraction. We desperately need to improve preaching and cultural sensitivity in the liturgy if the Church is to be attractive to Black Catholic Americans.

Fr. Giles A. Conwill, Ph.D. candidate, was ordained for the Diocese of San Diego in 1973. He was director of the Department of Church Vocations for the National Office for Black Catholics for four years. He has written articles on Black preaching, Black vocations, Black youth ministry, and Black music. His homilies have been published by *Homily Service* and by *The Upper Room.* He is completing work on a doctoral dissertation in cultural studies for Emory University, Atlanta.

WE SHARE . . . MINISTRY

Family Activities

We all say we want more black priests, brothers, sisters, lay ministers, bishops, deacons, popes. If we want them, we have to raise them and nurture them.

How can we as family:

promote vocations of service to God's people?

pray daily as family for vocations?

encourage all family members to participate in service projects sponsored by family, community, or Church?

welcome priests, brothers, sisters, deacons, and lay ministers into our homes to share life with us?

serve the people of God in church as a server, reader, usher, eucharistic minister, minister of the Word or of music?

If we want black vocations—bishops, priests, deacons, sisters, brothers, lay ministers—we have to raise them. Choose three things you as a family will do to foster vocations.

1.____________________

2.____________________

3.____________________

How can we as family minister to priests, brothers, sisters, lay ministers, deacons—in other words, to those who have dedicated their lives to the service of the Church?

CHD/Peter Magubane

How can we challenge them to be and to give their best?

How can we as family contribute to parish catechesis?

How can we as family share faith in our homes? How can we teach and learn the faith in our homes?

If our parish is multicultural, how can we as family ensure that catechesis is truly multicultural?

USCC/Nelson Brooks

WE SHARE . . . MINISTRY

Planning Christian Education in the Black Church

NATHAN W. JONES, PH.D.

1. BEGIN WITH YOUR VISIONS

What is it that we want the adults, youth, and children of our church—
to Know?
to Feel?
to Do?

2. STUDY YOUR CONGREGATION

Develop a membership file

- How many adults, youth, children are we addressing?
- What are these persons like?
- What is our larger community like?
- What is going on educationally in our parish?
- What are the strengths/weaknesses of our educational ministries?
- Where are the gaps in these programs?
- How are these programs organized?
- What financial resources are available?
- What leadership resources are available?

3. WHAT DO WE WISH TO DO?

- Initiate a process of study in order to explore the meaning of catechesis in the context of the needs of our local church.
- Set goals (what we wish to accomplish).
- Set objectives (how we wish to accomplish our goals).

4. EXPLORE EDUCATIONAL POSSIBILITIES

Study various ways of doing Christian education:

Wholistic: The total life, worship, preaching, witnessing, and service of the congregation is Christian education. Education and formation in faith is the responsibility of the total parish community. Catechesis builds on the life experiences of the people in their homes, in the streets, on their jobs, in their neighborhoods.

Inter-generational: Educational programming is organized across age lines. The entire parish community learns together in family clusters or learning teams. We live together not in separate communities because of generation, but rather, inter-age, and this should be reflected in our educational design.

Graded: Traditionally we have divided ages/groups based on the schooling model. However, there are certain times when a certain catechesis is more appropriate to a given age grouping than to another. This approach provides for this.

Learning Centers: A variety of creative learning activities are available to enable learners to accomplish the given aims of the catechesis in ways which are individually suitable.

Liberation-oriented Education: Learners are engaged in the transformation of their parish life by a process of critical reflection/action rooted in biblical faith and informed through catechesis. Persons are viewed as conscious beings and not objects. Persons are responsible for their personal growth in faith and the collective growth of the parish. Catechesis is aimed toward a converted life and a commitment to free the oppressed wherever they might be. Cathechists

Nathan W. Jones, Ph.D., is a consultant for religious education and pastoral ministry and an editor for Ethnic Communications Outlet in Chicago. He is author of a range of published resources for doing educational ministries in Black communities, including *Sharing the Old, Old Story: Educational Ministry in the Black Community* (St. Mary's Press).

enter into dialogue with the learners and view their role as ministers, enablers, resources.

5. EXPLORING TIMES AND SETTINGS

Sundays
- Sunday School
- Lectionary-based Bible study
- Liturgical season formation
- Afternoon learning experience

During the Week
- Midweek Bible study
- Released-time classes
- Storytelling experience
- After-school religious education/dinner
- At-home, at-church retreats
- Action-oriented learning; learning by doing

Vacation
- Bible school for all ages, which meets in evening and includes light supper/prayer/message/celebration.
- Church retreat in the country with opportunities for "down home" camp meetings, fellowship meals, Bible study, liturgy.

Bible and Culture School
- Catechesis and its relationship to Black heritage and culture is affirmed (e.g., one hour Bible/doctrine/liturgy; one hour of related Black cultural experiences. Integral relationship of faith and culture of the people).

Retreats
- Getaway days or weekends to pray can be excellent learning opportunities for all ages. Structured times for prayer, meals, creative learning can enable this time to be different from other learning situations in the church.
- Such retreats (or workshops) could be held in homes/senior citizens centers/church/retreat houses.

Congregational Meetings
- The entire parish community is invited to an information-sharing fellowship. News. Criticism. How we can collectively grow.

USCC/Nelson Brooks

6. HOW DO WE BUILD OUR CURRICULUM?
- Using and adapting existing materials: How can these tools enable us to achieve our catechetical goals more effectively? What changes will have to be made?
- Discovering new materials: Your local diocesan office of religious education provides services in the professional selection of teaching/learning materials.
- Developing our own curriculum: Organize around themes related to real life (such as crime/violence in the city, family life, economic power, identity), biblical story (how God has acted and is acting among his people), and Catholic-Christian tradition (unique ways we have of living, expressing, and witnessing that Jesus is Lord).

7. SELECTING RESOURCES
- People are the most vital resources.
- Role and function of resources.
- Varieties of resources available to church:

  people (speak with the elders, persons in pews with different talents, diocesan office personnel).

  institutional (other local churches, schools, area colleges, community centers, community organizations, and national organizations).

  materials (Bibles, books, periodicals, films, filmstrips, poetry, music, puppets, movies, TV, learning games).

8. ONGOING CATECHIST FORMATION

- Identification of gifted persons, trained as catechists, ministers of the Word.
- Support is offered these catechists through ongoing training sessions in local parish, in parish clusters, or on diocesan level.
- Times and occasions to celebrate the services of these catechists should be planned.
- Development of support services: home visitors, AV specialists.

9. EVALUATION

- Did we accomplish the goals originally set forth?
- Specify the ways and experiences through which these goals were accomplished.
- What are adults, youth, and children of our parish now thinking? Feeling? Doing?
- What are the most positive features of our education ministries? Why?
- What are the least admirable features of our programs? Why?
- What changes need to occur in our approach to Christian education; our models and programs, our teaching/learning techniques; our service efforts in the church and larger community; training of catechists; follow-up in the homes, school, community, parish life, liturgy, publicity, and personal contact.

USCC/Nelson Brooks

WE SHARE . . . MINISTRY

The Black Family Its Faith and Spirituality

NATHAN W. JONES, PH.D.

Once I visited an abandoned cemetery in Virginia which, I was told, had been the burial ground for the city's Black folk. I can vividly remember my surprise and anger upon seeing the neglect of the cemetery by the present generation. Hungry and untamed weeds grew everywhere. Many tombstones had either fallen or toppled over. There was a pervading feeling of abandonment.

I wondered how my generation, which talked so much about reclaiming our ancestral roots, could permit this hallowed burial ground, this Black Earth, to be forsaken.

I could almost hear the spirits of my unknown and unsung ancestors calling out. And I wanted to reply: "Speak to me of what you've seen, how you've lived. Tell me about your Journey. Tell me the story of my Blood so that I might pass it on."

I grew up in Indianapolis, Indiana and in Los Angeles, California in the midst of a colorful and prodigious family—an extended family.

My family easily could be compared to a beautiful house in which I've been weaned and nurtured. This house wasn't always neat and tidy because it was lived in. It even had broken windows, a sagging porch, and rusting pipes. But this house was built with love, and I knew it was mine.

From my family and people, I have received the breath of life. They taught me to question my world and to possess a passion for truth. These lessons have remained close to me ever since.

My people have so formed me that I can claim, define, and speak for myself: *I am an Afrikan Man. My cultural roots are in Mother Afrika, my fruits are in America; I am a religious man who confesses Jesus is Lord; I am a man determined to be free.*

My childhood was seasoned with some hardships in order to train me to travel rougher roads when I had to. My father split long ago. Uncles became "Dad" and taught my brother and me, through example, the meaning of manhood. I can even remember being hungry at times or without the money to do some of the things other children did in our neighborhood.

However, my family taught us long time ago that "trouble don't last always." This I have come to believe.

What do we as Black folk of faith believe about the experience of family? Is familyhood and the survival and stabilization of the family truly significant for us? What has been our personal experience of family? Who or what constitutes family for me today? When the poet, Nikki Giovanni, lifts up her voice singing, "Black love is Black wealth," what is the human experience she draws upon?

Each of us carries assumptions, hidden or revealed, about these questions. Our theology, ministries, our articulation and communication of the faith reflect these assumptions about family.

This word I seek to lift up is aimed toward enabling us together to explore the cultural richness of the Black family in the U.S. and the multiple shapes it takes.

We also aim toward exploring some of the myths, problems, and contemporary issues facing today's Black family within the context of Christian faith and spirituality.

The task before us is how creatively to enable persons in our various faith communities to build up, sustain, and transform the family. In a word, we are about an awesome yet a glorious adventure. . . .

CHD/Barbara Baker Stephenson

Nathan W. Jones, Ph.D., is a consultant for religious education and pastoral ministry and an editor for Ethnic Communications Outlet in Chicago. He is author of a range of published resources for doing educational ministries in Black communities, including *Sharing the Old, Old Story: Educational Ministry in the Black Community* (St. Mary's Press).

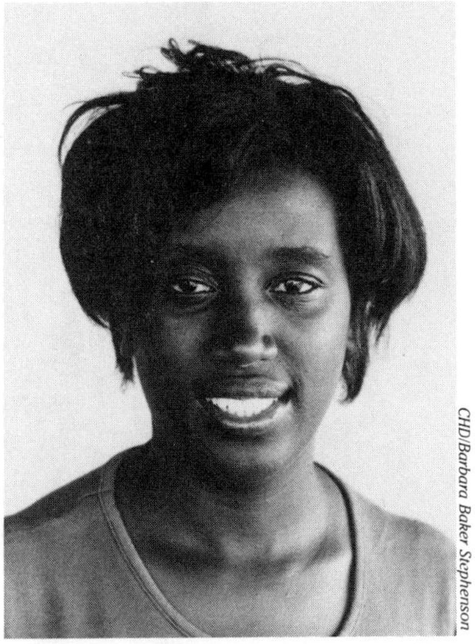
CHD/Barbara Baker Stephenson

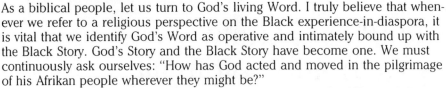

A BIBLICAL PERSPECTIVE ON FAMILY

As a biblical people, let us turn to God's living Word. I truly believe that whenever we refer to a religious perspective on the Black experience-in-diaspora, it is vital that we identify God's Word as operative and intimately bound up with the Black Story. God's Story and the Black Story have become one. We must continuously ask ourselves: "How has God acted and moved in the pilgrimage of his Afrikan people wherever they might be?"

The biblical term for family is closely related to our English word, *household.* Biblically speaking, household is a much broader term than what the nuclear family model implies–parents and children. When the biblical tradition speaks of household it is including everyone who lives together in one place or under one roof. Therefore, a household could include grandparents, in-laws, aunts, uncles, cousins, nieces, nephews, and even pets! Single persons, older couples, widows or widowers, two lovers also comprise a household, a family.

Drawing upon the insights of our biblical tradition as well as contemporary Black sociology, family is composed of any persons who live in relationship (usually in one household, under one roof). Using this broader definition, a family is any kind of household unity, covenant community or familial grouping. Families will include one-parent households with children, three generation families, couples without children, blended families of two adults with children from past marriages who have chosen to become a third family unit. Also, families will include single persons living alone; gay persons; families with foster children, retarded or handicapped members, or aging persons.

Of all the symbols of the Church, that of the family or more biblically accurate, the household, is the most attractive for a people seeking togetherness denied by the external forces of racism.

The New Testament Church as koinonia becomes a model of true family life. The sharing, fellowship, intimacy, covenant relationship, compassion, and network of care so characteristic of gospel living are the foundation principles of wholesome family life even for us today. No matter what shape family takes, these qualities of life together are at the root of meaningful relationships, with a view toward personal and collective growth and societal transformation.

No longer can we rely on the Adam/Eve image of family as functional for the contemporary Black Christian household. Rather, we must rediscover the biblical message and uncover its relevance for us, as our ancestors have taught through eloquent words and deeds.

MYTHS ABOUT THE BLACK FAMILY

Few human tragedies, not even the Jewish holocaust, equal the psychic destruction of a people as much as the Middle Passage, Afrikan slave trade experience. More than 250 million men, women, and children were killed. We lost scientists, master teachers, doctors, religious leaders. We lost the Black women who smothered their babies rather than subject them to enslavement. The Euro-Asian trade in slaves crippled the Black race and it was meant that we should never rise again. Our very soul, the spirit of our ancestors, the meaning of our existence, and the very purpose of our lives were eaten from us like skin from an antelope caught by a lion.

Therefore, when we reflect on ministry to the Black family in America, we must be prepared to encounter the strain and frustration, the racial, social, economic, political, and cultural oppression that Black people and Black families deal with daily in our relationships with one another and our world community. The destruction of a civilization lies in the ability of an alien people to disrupt the family. And it is not unreasonable to add that had not the redeeming action of God been present in our lives, enabling us to adapt and somehow overcome, any remnant of the Black family would have been totally destroyed as would have a total people.

The present-day Black family has inherited the legacy of our earliest days on these shores. One only needs to look at the number of Black men in prisons, the number of fatherless Black children and husbandless Black women, the unemployed Black men, to see that our family structure is at best precarious. In 1979 alone, 62 percent of the Black babies born in Chicago were of unmarried Black women. In 1978, half of all Black children born in the United States were of single Black women. We are up against a new phenomenon with untold implications for ministry.

Two tendencies have surrounded scholarship on the Black family. These are: (1) that the cultural retention of the Afrikan world view was radically destroyed by the Middle Passage and/or years of bondage; and (2) the horrors of the American experience have ultimately determined the nature of development of Black families.

In other words, scholarship has looked at the Black family only in comparison to the American standard, conceptual family—the white family. The Black family was conceived as only a "dark-skinned white family," an illegitimate white family.

What had resulted is the depiction of the Black family as disorganized, pathological, and almost nonexistent. Most research you will be exposed to points up the following themes: (1) Black families do not match the standard, conceptual white family; (2) that the original cultural and philosophical heritage of Black families was destroyed; and (3) that black families are "made in America."

Current research by Black psychologists and sociologists such as Robert Staples, Andrew Billingsley, and Wade Nobles rejects these assumptions and conclusions. To the contrary, it has been recognized that if Black people are to be truly free, we must begin to conceive of ourselves based upon *our own frame of reference, our own positives* rather than being defined and reacting to someone else's negatives.

Therefore, the Black family can only be fully understood when it is conceived of as a unit or system deriving its primary characteristics, forms, and definition from its Afrikan nature. This implies not simply one vision of family, but many possibilities of how the family unit might take shape, as well as a cultural continuity with our Afrikan roots.

STRENGTHS OF THE BLACK FAMILY AND IMPLICATIONS FOR MINISTRY

Despite the many death-like forces which have worked against the family, there stand forth many significant strengths which we must build on, at times judge, but always be conscious of.

The first of these strengths is *Black love.* It was love which enabled us to "look out for one another" and to take seriously the saying, "Blood is thicker than water." Most Black folk can recall the special warmth which characterized their households and most of us can say that our success and survival in life have depended in large measure on our family roots of love. Truly our greatest natural resource has been one another.

The story is told of the poet laureate of the state of Illinois, Gwendolyn Brooks. As a little girl, growing up in Topeka, Kansas, she frequently jotted verses of poetry on paper in various places in her family home. Spotting this budding talent in her daughter, Mrs. Keziah Brooks encouraged her daughter and saw to it that her gift with poetry was cultivated. Perhaps it was because the Brooks' household values such things as books, mealtimes, learning, and conversation, but Gwendolyn found in her family the motivation she needed to establish a literary career which has benefitted and enriched the whole world.

CHD/Peter Magubane

The most important area of family ministry in the Black community is the development and enhancement of self-worth, identity, purpose, and direction. This feeling about ourselves and those like us, is the foundation block for the individual, for the family, and the larger society.

Concretely, as Black Catholics we must seriously examine how our liturgical, education, and servant ministries, as well as our life together call forth the best in our people.

Ask yourself: Can I identify four key Black lay leaders in my Church or church-related institutions? What are the criteria I use to determine these leaders? What qualities do I look for in leaders in my Church? How am I facilitating the leadership development of my people in the life of the Church? Where in my Church is significant Black male leadership evident in decision-making roles? How is this leadership recognized in the community and honored? Are the Black leaders in my Church accountable to Black people or only to the white ministers? Is there a conscious effort on my part to identify and support emerging new leaders while opening new paths for old leaders? Do the Black male and female leadership see their roles as complementary or competitive?

A second strength of the Black family is its capacity to *extend itself,* to include and affirm rather than to exclude and deny. The extended family is that human involvement of families with families, where no child is without a mother or a father, and no grandparent is without a son or daughter, where all is shared and we take care of each other. The basis of the extended family is once more and again, love.

The extended family solves many problems. It is secure. When one eats, all eat. If one has a house to live in, all have a house to live in. Most of the needs of the members of the family are met by the family, such as care of the aged, seeing that all children have a mother and father. Single parenting is acceptable nowadays since white, suburban folk are doing it on a large scale. When only Black people experienced this reality, white researchers spoke of "illegitimacy," "fatherless children," or more harshly of "bastards." How quickly the rules of the game change, especially when somebody else writes the rules!

Christian faith is not so much taught as it is caught. We "catch" nurturant patterns and belief behaviors from others through a process called modeling. Religious educator, John H. Westerhoff III states that "true community necessitates the presence and interaction of three generations." The older generation is the one of tradition and memory. The middle-age generation is that of the present, dealing with everyday questions of "here and now." The youngest generation is the one of vision and hope.

Contemporary catechetical directives point to family as the most real and viable context for the religious education of adults, youth, and children today, or always. However, the question arises: given our insights into the complexities of today's Black family and extended family, how can we continue to use white catechetical materials and models, which are largely dysfunctional for Blacks, and seek effectively to form persons in faith?

I would like to propose that our catechetical ministries being to consider a model of catechesis based on households, the extended family, including all the generations. This model could be termed "community-as-educator" model and is based on the fact that everyone in one's household, or within one's circle of significant others, has a primary role in one's growth in faith. How can we network family members so that we meet them on the avenues where they are with a life-giving Word?

When we speak of family ministry in the Black parish, we must refer to all those relationships that are significant and formative in the lives of persons: home, community, institutions, the streets, the Church.

A third strength of the Black family is its *adaptability,* its versatility, especially as regards family roles. My Mamma could play a leading role in our family and *still* be a woman.

This kind of adaptability we must be attuned to in every aspect of our ministry. How rigid we are with liturgical guidelines and, in effect, hinder the spiritual growth of our people. How much do we seek to be acceptable to whites rather than take an unpopular stand and walk with our people? How seldom do we ever go to our own people, sit down and learn from them rather than always dominating, controlling, presiding, and being honored ourselves? It is strange how a people so creative and adaptable can become so unreflexive while our churches die and our people are left thirsting.

A fourth strength of the Black family is its *spirituality.* How many times have Momma's and Daddy's prayers and love travelled with us along the way? Our families were the places where we traditionally learned the values which lie at the heart of our people.

The Second Vatican Council as well as the Apostolic Exhortation, "Evangelization in the Modern World," both refer to the household as the "domestic Church." I firmly believe that basic communities of adults, youth, and children celebrating, learning, and serving are at the core of the life of the Church.

Small, visible units, within which the Gospel can be proclaimed and practiced, are central to the Church. Basic communities that are supportive of the household, the domestic Church, and individual persons within the community are essential to total religious education. This is "womb to tomb." The key is adults willing to share their faith and life with the next generation; for such is the history of the Church.

Drawing upon the spirituality that looms in every dimension of our lives, catechists and pastoral ministers must enable Black households to relearn the value of family prayer. Consecrate family Bibles, bless homes with incense and water made fragrant with spices, meet in homes for simple prayer services led by the head of the household or an elder followed by a love feast.

CHD/Lou Niznik

Provide opportunities in the life of your parish to celebrate in ritual/song/dance, a child's naming, engagement, healing and support in times of family crisis (whether economic or material); celebrations for those moving from adolescence to provisional adulthood; celebrations for those moving to a new parish. Honor graduates, retirees, and the mothers and fathers of your church. Our churches must also teach our people how to celebrate life's cycles in simple yet meaningful ways. In order to do so, we must teach folk the value of conversation and family meals over the blaring TV, bebopping stereo and TV dinners. Help folk learn to pray, maybe after meals when the noise has died down, Kool-aid has been wiped up, and everyone has arrived at the table.

We must search out new Sacraments, encounters with the divine, that emerge out of the Black experience. Do not be afraid to canonize them; nobody else will. Celebrate a love feast with cornbread and apple cider; use your buildings for family reunions or an elder/pioneer day.

Given the psychological pressures on families and family members, how can our churches more effectively minister?

The Association of Black Psychologists recently concluded, in a study of Black mental health in the urban community, that most Black people will more readily go to their churches and clergypersons for guidance, direction and counsel than to their local neighborhood free mental health facility. Why does this exist? The church environment has traditionally been a place where Black people have felt at home, comfortable, nonthreatened. The Black Church has been a place of nurturance which has sustained us through our life crises and joined with us in the celebration of our joys. I cannot think of a more natural place to begin our ministries toward Black family empowerment.

A word about our ministries to youth in the Black community: The goal of our youth ministry is to initiate our youth further into the life of the adult believing community and *not* into athletes, dancers, or theologians! Many urban churches place such a heavy emphasis on sports leagues, dance classes, disco, rather than concentrating on the meaningful integration of the youth into the life/worship/message/service of the total Church.

Everything I am saying keeps pointing back to and flowing out of Sunday morning, 11 o'clock—that eschatological moment when we meet God face-to-face. Worship should be the *best* service we offer the Black community. Unfortunately, many Catholic worship services are actually a *disservice* to Black people. Black folk of faith have traditionally *expected* the Church to provide this spiritual life, this nurture, this energy. If we cannot receive what we need for the battlefields of our lives, if we are not satisfied on Sundays, we'll search out satisfaction elsewhere. And the harsh reality is that we often go to places of death searching for *life.*

There is hope. Black people have survived the Middle Passage, the buffalo, the racist white missionaries. As dim as the sun's rays are, the will remains to conquer this oppressive and impersonal world. We must very carefully examine current values and our ministries. People—children included—should be foremost in our minds and hearts. Sound, healthy, life-giving, loving relationships are the foundation upon which a happy and fruitful life rests.

"The Black Family: Its Faith and Spirituality," Nathan Jones, originally published in PACE (*Professional Approaches for Christian Education*), Vol. 14 (October 1983).

PART V

Spreading the Word

What We Have Seen and Heard

EXCERPTS FROM A PASTORAL LETTER ON EVANGELIZATION FROM THE BLACK BISHOPS OF THE UNITED STATES

. . . We, the ten black bishops of the United States, chosen from among you to serve the people of God, are a significant sign among many other signs that the black Catholic community in the American Church has now come of age. We write to you as brothers that "you may share life with us." We write also to all those who by their faith make up the people of God in the United States that "our joy may be complete." And what is this joy? It is that joy that the Ethiopian eunuch, the treasurer of the African queen, expressed in the Book of Acts when he was baptized by the deacon, Philip: He "went on his way rejoicing" (Acts 8:39). We rejoice because, like this African court official, we, the descendants of Africans brought to these shores, are now called to share our faith and to demonstrate our witness to our risen Lord.

We write to you, black brothers and sisters, because each one of us is called to a special task. The Holy Spirit now calls us all to the work of evangelization. As he did for Peter, the Lord Jesus has prayed for us that our faith might not fail (Lk 22:32), and with Paul we all are compelled to confess: "Yet preaching the Gospel is not the subject of a boast; I am under compulsion and have no choice. I am ruined if I do not preach it!" (1 Cor 9:16).

Evangelization is both a call and a response. It is the call of Jesus reverberating down the centuries: "Go into the whole world and proclaim the good news to all creation" (Mk 16:15). The response is, "Conduct yourselves, then, in a way worthy of the Gospel of Christ" (Phil 1:27). Evangelization means not only preaching but witnessing; not only conversion but renewal; not only entry into the community but the building up of the community; not only hearing the word but sharing it. Evangelization, said Pope Paul VI, "is a question not only of preaching the Gospel in ever wider geographic areas or to ever greater numbers of people, but also of affecting and as it were upsetting, through the power of the Gospel, mankind's criteria of judgment, determining values, points of interest, lines of thought, sources of inspiration and models of life, which are in contrast with the Word of God and the plan of salvation."[1]

Pope Paul VI issued that call to the peoples of Africa when he said to them at Kampala in Uganda, "You are now missionaries to yourselves." And Pope Paul also laid out for all sons and daughters of Africa the nature of the response, "You must now give your gifts of blackness to the whole Church."[2]

We believe that these solemn words of our Holy Father Paul VI were addressed not only to Africans today but also to us, the children of the Africans of yesterday. We believe that the Holy Father has laid a challenge before us to share the gift of our blackness with the Church in the United States. This is a challenge to be evangelizers, and so we want to write about this gift, which is also a challenge. First, we shall write about the gifts we share, gifts rooted in our African heritage. Then we will write about the obstacles to evangelization that we must still seek to overcome . . . .

CHD/Peter Magubane

THE FAMILY

(Cf. *Evangelii Nuntiandi,* 71.)

The heart of the human community is the family. In our society today, traditional family values are openly questioned and rejected. For many reasons the black family has been especially assailed, despite the importance that families still have in the black cultural and spiritual tradition.

For us the family has always meant "the extended family"—the grandparents, the uncles and aunts, the godparents, all those related by kinship or strong friendship. This rich notion of family was not only part of an African tradition but also was our own African-American experience. Child care became the responsibility of many persons, for necessity demanded that many share the labor, distribute the burden and, yes, even the joy.

In practice, the extended family often goes beyond kinship and marital relationship to include persons who, having no family of their own, have been accepted into the wider family circle. These family members feel a deep responsibility for one another in both ordinary times of daily life and in the extraordinary moments of need or crisis.

It is for this reason that, despite the erosion of family life among us, we as a people continue to have a strong sense of family bonds. In its Christian setting this family sense enhances the role of godparents and other relatives who must often shoulder the responsibility for passing on the faith and strengthening the religious values of the young. Moreover, there is more than one priestly or religious vocation among us that was nurtured by the support and encouragement of some adult in the extended family. Not infrequently, young blacks in the seminary or religious-formation house have been informally adopted by a sponsor or have been welcomed into the circle of a second family.

CHD/Peter Magubane

This sense of family in our own African-American tradition can easily be translated into a richer sense of Church as a great and all-embracing family. In our parishes, we should truly look upon ourselves as brothers and sisters to one another. The elders among us should be a living resource for the young, for they have much to tell and teach. Our celebrations should be the affirmation of our kinship and our common bond. The words of the third Eucharistic Prayer, "Father, hear the prayers of the family you have gathered here before you," are not a pious fiction but a sacred reality that defines the meaning of the Catholic community. In a word, evangelization for black Catholics is a celebration of the family, a renewal of the family, and a call to welcome new members into the family of God.

THE ROLE OF BLACK MEN

(Cf. *Evangelii Nuntiandi,* 73, 76.)

Central to any discussion of the black family today is the question of the black man as husband, father, coprovider and coprotector. For many historical reasons, the black man has been forced to bear the crushing blows of racial hate and economic repression. Too often barred from access to decent employment, too often stripped of his dignity and manhood, and too often forced into a stereotype that was a caricature of his manhood, the black male finds himself depreciated and relegated to the margins of family life and influence. Not the least of the evil fruits of racial segregation has been the artificially fashioned rivalry between black women and men.

It is important, we believe, to encourage a reevaluation of the fundamental vocation to fatherhood that black men must have in the context of the black family. In our cultural heritage, the father provides the courage and wisdom to help maintain the family and to ensure its growth. We challenge black men of today to assert their spiritual strength and to demonstrate their sense of responsibility and ethnic pride. We call upon black men to become what their fathers were—even when an evil institution sought to destroy their individuality and their initiative—that is, models of virtue for their children and partners in love and nurturing with their wives. Without a father, no family life can be fully complete. Let the black father find his model in the fatherhood of God, who by his providence nourishes us, who by his wisdom guides us, and who by his love cherishes us and makes us all one and holy in his family of grace."

THE ROLE OF WOMEN

(Cf. *Evangelii Nuntiandi,* 73,76.)

The civil rights movement of the 1960s that we as a people initiated and in which we suffered raised the consciousness of many people to the reality of social inequities and social injustice. In many ways our struggle served as a pattern and model for others who were made aware of their own plight. Within the last decade we all have become more conscious of the social inequities that women as a group have suffered and continue to suffer in our society. In a very special way, these inequities weigh most heavily on black women and women of other racial minorities.

On the other hand, black women have had and continue to have a place within the black community that is unique. In traditional black society, women have had to assume responsibilities within the family and within the community out of necessity. As a result, black women historically have been not only sources of strength, they also have been examples of courage and resolution. This strength and courage are for us all a source of power and a powerful gift that we as a people can share with the larger society.

The role of black women within the context of black history, however, has not been a subordinate role to black men, but a complementary role. Women like Sojourner Truth, Harriet Tubman, and Mary McLeod Bethune were heirs of an African tradition.

If this is true of the African-American tradition, it is even more so for we who are the heirs of a black Catholic tradition. Before there were black Catholic priests in the United States, there were black women religious. The challenge of evangelization within the black Catholic community was taken up by four black women in the hostile environment of Baltimore, under the leadership of Elizabeth Lange. The Church gave approval to her work when the Oblate Sisters of Providence were officially recognized as a religious congregation in 1831. Evangelization among the blacks of New Orleans was also the task assumed by Henriette Delille, who in the face of crushing opposition founded the Sisters of the Holy Family in 1842. These two black congregations of religious women were joined by a third in our own century when Mother Theodore Williams helped establish the Franciscan Handmaids of the Most Pure Heart of Mary in 1916 in Savannah, Georgia.

CHD/Peter Magubane

These black women religious leaders and the sisters whom they formed were not only witnesses of faith; they were also a sign of the faith of many black Catholic families who, even in the dark days of slavery, gave not only support, but even their daughters and sisters in the service of the Gospel.

Within the black Catholic community today, black women continue to witness in various nonordained ministries, both as religious and lay. This ministry is to be found on the parochial and the diocesan level. It is a ministry in schools and in the social apostolate. Needless to say, this potential for service within our own community needs to be more fully recognized and utilized by the Catholic Church in the United States. Black women can and should be considered as collaborators in the work of evangelization. The words of the pastoral commission of the Congregation for the Evangelization of Peoples are eminently true of women in the black Catholic community: "Givers of life, consecrated by nature to its service, it is for women to give to evangelization a living and realistic face before the world."[3]

ABORTION AND BLACK VALUES

(Cf. *Evangelii Nuntiandi,* 65.)

Today the black family is assailed on all sides. Much has been said by others about the economic plight of the black family. We would like to add a word regarding the moral aspect of this plight.

The acceptance of abortion by many as a common procedure and even as a right is a reality not only in our American society as a whole, but also within the black community. And yet life, and especially new life within the mother, has always been a value to Africans and to African-Americans. Historically, even children conceived outside of marriage were cherished and given a place in the extended family. Black cultural tradition has always valued life and the mystery of its transmission and growth. Children have always been for us a sign of hope. The loss of this perspective is a cultural and spiritual impoverishment for us as a people.

From our point of view as Catholics and as black people, we see the efforts made "to provide" low-cost abortions as another form of subjugation. Indeed there are those who would even characterize it as a form of genocide. As a people of faith, it is our task to fight for the right to life of all our children and in all the circumstances of their existence. It is our duty to reassert the gift of our traditional African-American values of family and children to our own people and to our society as a whole. It is equally our duty, however, to show practical concern and honest compassion for the many mothers-to-be who are too often encouraged to seek an abortion by the conventional wisdom of our society today.

Finally, we add this unfortunate observation: If society truly valued our children and our mothers—mothers who have already made a choice for life—they would have day-care centers, jobs, good schools, and all else that a just society should offer to its people. Sadly, we observe that if abortion were abolished tomorrow, the same disastrous ills would plague our black mothers and children.

NOTES

1. Pope Paul VI, *On Evangelization in the Modern World* (Washington, D.C.: USCC Office of Publishing and Promotion Services, 1975), no. 19.

2. The actual words of Pope Paul VI are the following:

"If you are able to avoid the possible dangers of religious pluralism, the danger of making your Christian profession into a kind of local folklore, or into exclusivist racism, or into egoistic tribalism or arbitrary separatism, then you will be able to remain sincerely African even in your own interpretation of the Christian life; you will be able to formulate Catholicism in terms congenial to your own culture; you will be capable of bringing to the Catholic Church the precious and original contribution of 'negritude,' which she needs particularly in this historic hour." "To the Heart of Africa," (address to the Bishops of the African Continent at the closing session of a symposium held in Kampala, Uganda). In *The Pope Speaks* 14, (1969), 219.

3. Pastoral Commission of the Congregation for the Evangelization of Peoples, *The Role of Women in Evangelization, Vatican II: More Postconciliar Documents*. Austin Flannery, OP, general editor (Northport, N.Y.: 1982), 327. (Note: A study guide for this pastoral is available from the Josephite Pastoral Center, 1200 Varnum Street, N.E., Washington, D.C. 20017.

The Catholic Standard/*Michael Hoyt*

Left to right, standing: Auxiliary Bishop Wilton Gregory of Chicago, Auxiliary Bishop Emerson Moore of New York, Auxiliary Bishop Moses Anderson of Detroit, Auxiliary Bishop J. Terry Steib of St. Louis, Auxiliary Bishop John Ricard of Baltimore; seated: Auxiliary Bishop Joseph Francis of Newark, Auxiliary Bishop Harold Perry of New Orleans, Bishop Joseph Howze of Biloxi, Auxiliary Bishop Eugene Marino of Washington, D.C., Auxiliary Bishop James Lyke of Cleveland.

Resolutions on Family

NATIONAL OFFICE FOR BLACK CATHOLICS CONFERENCE, CHICAGO, 1980

We see the need to develop more cohesiveness in Black Family Life through the Mystical Body of Christ which embraces all the People of God. Despite the historical strengths of black family ties, there are today societal pressures that are fragmenting the structure of the black family.

The philosophies of materialism, individualism, and secularism are undercutting the fabric of family life based upon fidelity and commitment. We see this in the alarming figures on divorce, domestic violence and abuse, challenges to authority, and the general breakdown in moral values.

In addressing some of these concerns we present the following resolutions:

CHD/Lou Niznik

A. STABILITY IN FAMILY LIFE

Be It Resolved That:

- Each parish develop a strong premarital instruction program for black couples seeking marriage in the Catholic Church. (Black married couples should be used in counseling.)
- Priests, deacons, or sisters involved must be knowledgeable, trained, and sensitive to the unique problems of black couples and the dynamics between black males and females.
- Programs such as the "Engaged Encounter" and "Marriage Encounter" be made relevant to the Black Experience.
- Catholic clergy be trained in the psychology and culture of Black Family Life.
- Parishes be encouraged to develop family-couple support groups to help sustain the family and enhance Christian values.
- The parish should actively involve itself in supporting the development of family prayer groups.
- Efforts be made to initiate and continue creating a place in the parish Christian community for divorced persons and their families.
- Members of each parish be specially trained to counsel parish members in times of family crisis such as: death, mental illness, substance abuse, incarceration, and teen-age pregnancy. (These committees of parish members should be linked to social service agencies and other resources within the community, and each diocese should set up a fund to share as needed with parishes for use in aiding families with financial crisis.)

B. KEEPING FAMILIES IN THE CHURCH/BRINGING THEM BACK

Be It Resolved That:

- Pastoral staff members and parishioners of the Catholic community initiate a program of "Reaching Out" to all black families.
- The style of the liturgy should vary to meet the needs of the parishioners, such as Gospel, Latin, Youth, etc.
- The social and service activities of the parish should be so planned by the staff and parish representatives (parish council) that they "reach out" to people of all age levels, both present members and newcomers. (Examples of these are programs for "welcome" systems, "youth ministry," and various support groups.)
- NOBC convene on a bi-annual basis a national conclave and on alternate years a regional convention. It is good for this (black Catholic) family to have face-to-face communications at regular intervals.

C. DEVELOPING COHESIVENESSS WITHIN THE FAMILY

In order to rekindle those effective family parenting styles of prior generations which could successfully be implemented in the parish, community, and family,

Be It Resolved That:

- Family members establish a line of open communication with each other.
- Black Family Life be addressed through liturgical, sacramental, and social ministries in each parish.
- Black studies be developed within the parish and school.
- Family members develop new forms of expressing their commitment of love.
- The family rededicate its members to the meaning of family life.
- The Church (parish) initiate a program of family-life education as part of regular parish catechetical programs.
- Personalized means to be devised to increase the male participation in home, school, and church activities.
- Parishes develop activities for the total family.

Whereas, In the black tradition respect and loyalty for each member of the household is paramount along with knowing that God is Love, **We Resolve** to bolster within ourselves and within others the commitment of *self* totally to God to enable us to see God in ourselves and in others, reclaiming and proclaiming within the whole Christian family that Jesus Christ is Lord.

USCC/Nelson Brooks

AMENDMENTS

Be it Resolved, That the National Conference of Catholic Bishops make explicit the definition of family to include that broad concept of household: the nuclear family, the single parent (male or female), the school-age parent, siblings living together, divorced persons, interracial or interfaith spouses, so that values can be assimilated through that family's community environment.

Whereas, There has been a history of forced breeding and rape of black women during slavery; and

Whereas, The word "illegitimate" means no rights to inherit from the father; and

Whereas, This lack of responsibility has been the basis for intergenerational poverty; and

Whereas, It is consistent with our African Heritage that these children shall be accepted and claimed by all black people in the extended black family through advocacy, formal and informal adoption.

Be it Resolved, That we reject the use of this word rightly and that the NBLCC and NOBC urge the Congress of the United States to abolish all legal impediments attached to all persons born out of wedlock to entitle such persons to all rights and privileges accorded children born to wedded parents.

"Resolutions on Family," *Black Catholics: Architects of an Action Agenda for the '80s,* IMPACT! Vol. X, Nos. 8–10 (August–October 1980). Copyright © 1980 National Office for Black Catholics, Washington, D.C. Reprinted with permission.

PART VI

Appendix

Black Catholic Resource Centers

All of these centers provide human as well as print and/or media resources for the Black Catholic family.

Academy of the Afro-World Community
Box C
Detroit, Michigan 48213

Black Liturgy Subcommittee of the Bishops' Committee on the Liturgy
National Conference of Catholic Bishops
1312 Massachusetts Avenue, N.W.
Washington, D.C. 20005

Ethnic Communications Outlet
5342 S. University Avenue
Chicago, Illinois 60615

Josephite Pastoral Center
1200 Varnum Street, N.E.
Washington, D.C. 20017

Knights of Peter Claver and Ladies' Auxiliary
Claver Building
1825 Orleans Avenue
New Orleans, Louisiana 70116

Media Production Center
Society of the Divine Word
Ulman Avenue
Bay St. Louis, Mississippi 39520

National Association of Black Catholic Administrators
c/o Mrs. Dolores Morgan
807 Onodoga Avenue
Syracuse, New York 13207

National Black Catholic Clergy Caucus
1419 V Street, N.W.
Suite 400
Washington, D.C. 20009

National Black Catholic Seminarians' Association
c/o National Black Catholic Clergy Caucus
1419 V Street, N.W.
Suite 400
Washington, D.C. 20009

National Black Lay Catholic Caucus
810 Rhode Island Avenue, N.E.
Washington, D.C. 20018

National Black Sisters' Conference
6226 Camden Street
Oakland, California 94605

National Office for Black Catholics
810 Rhode Island Avenue, N.E.
Washington, D.C. 20018

Stimuli, Inc.
Fr. Clarence Jos. Rivers, Jr., Ph.D.
17 Erkenbrecher Avenue
Cincinnati, Ohio 45220

Collections of Black Religious Songs

American Negro Folk-Songs. Newman Ivey White. 1928. Reprinted Hatboro, Pa.: Folklore Associates, 1965.

American Negro Songs and Spirituals. John W. Work. New York: Bonanza Books, 1940.

The Best of James Cleveland. Sallie Martin and Kenneth Morris, comp. Chicago: Martin and Morris Music, Inc., 1965. Collection of gospel songs written by James Cleveland.

The Book of American Negro Spirituals. James Weldon Johnson, and J. Rosamond Johnson. 2 vols. 1926–27. Reprinted New York: Da Capo Press, 1977.

Dorsey's Songs of the Kingdom. Thomas Dorsey and others, comp. Chicago: Thomas A. Dorsey, 1951. Collection of gospel songs written by Thomas Dorsey.

Dorsey's Songs with a Message. Thomas Dorsey and others, comp. Chicago: Thomas A. Dorsey, 1951. Collection of gospel songs written by Thomas Dorsey.

Just Andrae! Andrae Crouch. Waco, Texas: Lexicon Music, 1972. Collection of gospel songs recorded by Andrae Crouch. Arranged for youth choirs.

Lift Every Voice and Sing. Compiled and edited by Irene V. Jackson. New York: The Church Hymnal Corporation, 1981. Includes spirituals and gospel music.

Slave Songs of the United States. William Allen; Charles Ware; and Lucy Garrison. New York: A. Simpson, 1867. Reprinted New York, 1967.

Songs of Zion. Compiled and edited by J. Jefferson Cleveland, and Verolga Nix. Preface by William B. McClain. Nashville: Abingdon Press, 1981. Includes contemporary and traditional gospel as well as spirituals.

Soulfully. Andrae Crouch. Waco, Texas: Lexicon Music, 1972. Collection of gospel songs recorded by Andrae Crouch. Arranged for choirs.

NOTE: For references to scores of music of black composers, see Evelyn Davidson White, *Selected Bibliography of Published Choral Music by Black Composers*, Metuchen, N.J.: Scarecrow Press, 1981.

RECORDED MUSIC

Deliver the Word. St. Augustine Gospel Choir, Leon C. Roberts, composer and director, 1985. Available in album and cassette from Roberts Publications, Inc., 1419 V Street, N.W., Washington, D.C. 20009.

God's Love Is Eternal and Everlasting. St. Teresa of Avila (Catholic) Gospel Choir, John E. Watson, producer and director, 1985. Available in album and cassette from P.O. Box 15245, Washington, D.C. 20003-0245.

He Has the Power: The Mass of St. Augustine. St. Augustine Gospel Choir, Leon C. Roberts, composer and director. (Chicago: Gregorian Institute of America, 1982). Available in album, cassette, and sheet music from Roberts Publications, Inc., 1419 V Street, N.W., Washington, D.C. 20009.

The Mass of St. Martin de Porres. St. Augustine Gospel Choir, Leon C. Roberts, composer and director, 1985. Available in album and cassette from Roberts Publications, Inc., 1419 V Street, N.W., Washington, D.C. 20009.

The Mass of St. Teresa of Avila. St. Teresa of Avila (Catholic) Gospel Choir, John E.Watson, producer and director, 1985. Available in album and cassette from P.O. Box 15245, Washington, D.C. 20003-0245.

Rejoice! A Conference on Black Catholic Liturgy. Archdiocese of Washington, Office of Black Catholics, 1984 and 1985. A full series of audio cassettes and video cassettes of concerts, keynote addresses, and liturgical highlights for both 1984 and 1985. Available from the Archdiocese of Washington, Office of Black Catholics, P.O. Box 29260. Washington, D.C. 20017.

A Working Bibliography on the Black Family in American Society

COMPILED BY TOINETTE M. EUGENE, PH.D.

BOOKS

Aschenbrenner, Joyce. "Continuities and Variations in Black Family Structure." In *The Extended Family in Black Societies,* edited by Demitri Shimkin, Edith M. Shimkin, and Dennis A. Frate, 181–200. The Hague: Mouton Publishers, 1978.

Bernard, Jessie. *Marriage and Family Among Negroes.* Englewood Cliffs, N.J.: Prentice-Hall, 1966.

Billingsley, Andrew. *Black Families and the Struggle for Survival.* New York: Friendship Press, 1974.

———. *Black Families in White America.* Englewood Cliffs, N.J.: Prentice-Hall, 1968.

Blackwell, James E. *The Black Community: Diversity and Unity.* New York: Dodd, Mead & Co., 1975.

Blassingame, John. *The Slave Community.* New York: Oxford University Press, 1972.

Clark, Kenneth B. *Dark Ghetto.* New York: Harper & Row, 1965.

Comer, James P., and Alvin F. Pouissant. *Black Child Care.* New York: Simon & Schuster, 1975.

Cone, James H. *Black Theology and Black Power.* New York: Seabury, 1969.

———. *God of the Oppressed.* New York: Seabury, 1975.

Davis, Lenwood G. *The Black Family in the United States: A Selected Bibliography of Annotated Books, Articles, and Dissertations on Black Families in America.* Westport, Conn.: Greenwood Press, 1978.

Dodson, Jualynne. "Conceptualizations of Black Families." In *Black Families,* edited by Harriet P. McAdoo, 23–36. Beverly Hills, Calif.: Sage Publications, 1981.

Drake, St. Clair, and Horace Cayton. *Black Metropolis.* New York: Harcourt, Brace & Co., 1945.

DuBois, W.E.B. *The Negro American Family.* Atlanta: Atlanta University Press, 1908.

———. *The Souls of Black Folk.* Greenwich, Conn.: Fawcett, 1961.

Faherty, William B., SJ, and Madeline B. Olivers. *The Religious Roots of Black Catholics in St. Louis.* St. Louis: St. Louis University Press, 1977.

Frazier, E. Franklin. *Black Bourgeoisie.* New York: Free Press, 1957.

———. *The Free Negro Family.* 1932. Reprint. New York: Arno Press, 1968.

———. *The Negro Church in America.* New York: Schocken Books, 1974.

———. *The Negro Family in Chicago.* Chicago: University of Chicago Press, 1932.

———. *The Negro Family in the United States.* Chicago: University of Chicago Press, 1939.

Gibson, William. *Family Life and Morality: Studies in Black and White.* Washington, D.C.: University Press of America, 1980.

Gillard, John T. *The Catholic Church and the American Negro.* Baltimore: Josephite Press, 1929.

———. *Colored Catholics in the United States.* Baltimore: Josephite Press, 1941.

Greeley, Andrew, ed. *The Family in Crisis or in Transition: A Sociological and Theological Perspective.* New York: Seabury, 1979.

Gutman, Herbert G. *The Black Family in Slavery and Freedom, 1750–1925.* New York: Pantheon Books, 1976.

Haley, Alex. *Roots: The Saga of an American Family.* Garden City, N.Y.: Doubleday & Co., 1976.

Heiss, Jerold. *The Case of the Black Family: A Sociological Inquiry.* New York: Columbia University Press, 1975.

Hill, Robert B. *The Strengths of Black Families.* New York: Emerson Hall Publishers, 1972.

———. *Black Families in the 1974–75 Depression: Special Policy Report.* New York: National Urban League, 1975.

John Paul II. *On the Family: Regarding the Role of the Christian Family in the Modern World* [*Familiaris Consortio*]. Washington, D.C.: United States Catholic Conference, 1982.

Kronus, Sidney J. *The Black Middle Class.* Columbus, Ohio: Charles E. Merrill, 1970.

Ladner, Joyce A. *Tomorrow's Tomorrow: The Black Woman.* Garden City, N.Y.: Doubleday & Co., 1971.

———. *Mixed Families: Adopting Across Racial Boundaries.* Garden City, N.Y.: Doubleday & Co., 1978.

Lenero-Otero, Luis, ed. *Beyond the Nuclear Family Model: Cross-Cultural Perspectives.* Beverly Hills, Calif.: Sage Publications, 1977.

Leslie, Gerard R. *The Family in Social Contact.* 5th ed. New York: Oxford University Press, 1982.

Lincoln, C. Eric. *The Black Church Since Frazier.* New York: Schocken Books, 1974.

———. *The Black Experience in Religion.* Garden City, N.Y.: Anchor Books, 1974.

Lyman, Stanford, M. *The Black American in Sociological Thought.* New York: G.P. Putnam's Sons, 1972.

McAdoo, Harriette P., ed. *Black Families.* Beverly Hills, Calif.: Sage Publications, 1981.

McCord, William, et al. *Life-Styles in the Black Ghetto.* New York: W.W. Norton & Co., 1969.

Martin, Elmer P., and Joanne Mitchell Martin. *The Black Extended Family.* Chicago: University of Chicago Press, 1978.

May, Benjamin E., and Joseph W. Nicholson. *The Negro's Church.* New York: Institute of Social and Religious Research, 1933.

Minuchin, Salvador, et al. *Families of the Slums.* New York: Basic Books, 1967.

Moyd, Olin P. *Redemption in Black Theology.* Valley Forge, Pa.: Judson Press, 1979.

Moynihan, Daniel Patrick. *The Negro Family: The Case for National Action.* Washington, D.C.: U.S. Government Printing Office, 1965.

Myrdal, Gunnar. *An American Dilemma: The Negro Problem and Modern Democracy.* New York: Harper & Row, 1944.

National Office for Black Catholics. *Black Perspectives on Evangelization in the Modern World.* Washington, D.C.: NOBC, 1974.

Nelsen, Hart M., and Anne K. Nelsen. *Black Church in the Sixties.* Lexington: University of Kentucky Press, 1975.

Nelsen, Hart M.; Raytha L. Yokley; Anne K. Nelsen. *The Black Church in America.* New York: Basic Books, 1971.

Osborne, William. *The Segregated Covenant: Race Relations and American Catholics.* New York: Herder and Herder, 1967.

Parsons, Talcott, and Kenneth B. Clark, eds. *The Negro American.* Boston: Houghton Mifflin Co., 1966.

Peters, Marie F. "Parenting in Black Families with Young Children: A Historical Perspective." In *Black Families,* edited by Harriette P. McAdoo, 211–17. Beverly Hills, Calif.: Sage Publications, 1981.

Pinkney, Alphonso. *Black Americans.* Englewood Cliffs, N.J.: Prentice-Hall, 1975.

Polski, Harry A., and James Williams, eds. *The Afro-American: The Negro Reference Almanac.* 4th ed. New York: John Wiley & Sons, 1983.

Raboteau, Albert J. *Slave Religion.* New York: Oxford University Press, 1978.

Rainwater, Lee and William L. Yancey. *The Moynihan Report and the Politics of Controversy.* Cambridge: MIT Press, 1967.

Roberts, J. Deotis. *A Black Political Theology.* Philadelphia: Westminster Press, 1974.

———. *Liberation and Reconciliation: A Black Theology.* Philadelphia: Westminster Press, 1975.

———. *Roots of a Black Future: Family and Church.* Philadelphia: Westminster Press, 1980.

Scanzoni, John H. *The Black Family in Modern in Modern Society: Patterns of Stability and Security.* Boston: Allyn & Bacon, 1971.

Schulz, David A. *The Changing Family: Its Function and Its Future.* Englewood Cliffs, N.J.: Prentice-Hall, 1972.

———. *Coming Up Black: Patterns of Ghetto Socialization.* Englewood Cliffs, N.J.: Prentice Hall, 1969.

Schuster, George, SSJ, and Robert M. Kearns, SSJ. *Statistical Profile of Black Catholics.* Washington, D.C.: Josephite Press, 1975.

Sheehan, Arthur, and Elizabeth Sheehan. *Pierre Toussaint: Citizen of Old New York.* New York: P.J. Kenedy & Sons, 1955.

Shimkin, Demitri; Edith M. Shimkin; and Dennis A. Frate, eds. *The Extended Family in Black Societies.* The Hague: Mouton Publishers, 1978.

Stack, Carol B. *All Our Kin: Strategies for Survival in a Black Community.* New York: Harper & Row, 1974.

Staples, Robert. *The Black Family: Essays and Studies.* Belmont, Calif.: Wadsworth Publishing Co., 1971.

———. *Introduction to Black Sociology.* New York: McGraw-Hill, 1976.

———. *The Black Woman in America: Sex, Marriage, and the Family.* Chicago: Nelson-Hall Publishers, 1973.

Thomas, George B. *Young Black Adults: Liberation and Family Attitudes.* New York: Friendship Press, 1974.

Thompson, Daniel C. *Sociology of the Black Experience.* Westport, Conn.: Greenwood Press, 1974.

Whitehead, Evelyn E., and James D. Whitehead. *Marrying Well: Possibilities in Christian Marriage Today.* Garden City, N.Y.: Doubleday & Co., 1981.

Willie, Charles V., ed. *The Family Life of Black People.* Columbus, Ohio: Charles E. Merrill, 1970.

———. *A New Look at Black Families.* Bayside, N.Y.: General Hall, 1981.

Wilmore, Gayraud S., and James H. Cone, eds., *Black Theology: A Documentary History, 1966–1979.* Maryknoll, N.Y.: Orbis Books, 1979.

Wimberly, Edward P. *Pastoral Counseling and Spiritual Values: A Black Point of View.* Nashville: Abingdon Press, 1982.

———. *Pastoral Care in the Black Church.* Nashville: Abingdon Press, 1979.

Woodson, G. Carter. *The History of the Negro Church.* Washington, D.C.: Associated Publishers, 1921.

ARTICLES

Allen, Walter R. "The Search for Applicable Theories of Black Family Life." *Journal of Marriage and the Family* 40 (February 1978): 117–29.

America (March 29, 1980): Entire issue devoted to "Black Catholics and Their Church."

Andersen, Kurt. "A Threat to the Future: Coming to Grips with the Crumbling Black Family." *Time* (May 14, 1984):20.

Billingsley, Andrew. "Black Families and National Policy." *Journal of Sociology and Social Welfare* 2 (Spring 1975): 312–25.

———. "Black Families and White Social Science." *Journal of Social Issues* 26 (November 1975): 127–42.

Braxton, Edward K. "The Black Catholic Experience in America." *Origins* 10 (January 22, 1981): 497–502.

Clarke, John Henrik. "The History of the Black Family." *Journal of Afro-American Issues* 3 (Summer/Fall 1975): 336–42.

Collins, Daniel F. "Black Conversion to Catholicism: Its Implications for the Negro Church." *Journal for the Scientific Study of Religion* 10 (Fall 1971): 208–18.

Comer, James P. "Single Parent Black Families." *The Crisis* 90 (December 1983): 42–47.

Davis, Cyprian, OSB. "Black Catholics in America: A Historical Note." *America* 142 (May 3, 1980): 377–78.

———. "The Catholic Church in the Black Community Today: A General Overview." *City of God* 2 (Summer 1980): 32–38.

Davis, Joseph M., SM. "The Position of the Catholic Church in the Black Community." *Freeing the Spirit* 1 (Summer 1972): 18–24.

Dennis, Rutledge. "Theories of the Black Family: The Weak Family and the Strong Family Schools as Competing Ideologies." *Journal of Afro-American Issues* 4 (Summer/Fall 1976): 315–28.

Hale, Janice. "The Woman's Role: The Strength of Black Families." *First World* 1 (March/April 1977): 28–30.

Hare, Nathan. "What Black Intellectuals Misunderstand about the Black Family." *Black World* 25 (March 1976): 4–14.

Jones, Nathan. "Making It Plain: Affirmations for Black Family Ministry." *Pass It On* 1, no. 3 (1983): 4.

Lumas, Eva Marie. "Parents and Church as Educators." *Pass It On* 1 no. 3 (1983): 2–3.

McAdoo, Harriette P. "Factors Related to Stability in Upwardly Mobile Black Families." *Journal of Marriage and the Family* 40 (November 1978): 761–76.

———. "Impact of the Extended Family Structure on Upward Mobility of Blacks." *Journal of Afro-American Issues* 3 (Summer/Fall 1975): 291–96.

Nobles, Wade W. "Africanity: Its Role in Black Families." *The Black Scholar* 5 (June 1974): 10–17.

———. "African Root and American Fruit: The Black Family." *The Journal of Social and Behavioral Sciences* 20 (Spring 1974): 66–77.

———. "Toward an Empirical and Theoretical Framework for Defining Black Families." *Journal of Marriage and the Family* 40 (November 1978): 679–90.

Peters, Marie F., ed. "Special Issue: Black Families." *Journal of Marriage and the Family* 40 (November 1978): 667–828.

Sarpong, Peter. "The African Family at the Synod." *CRUX of the News* (October 27, 1980): 4–5.

Staples, Robert. "The Black Family in Evolutionary Perspective." *Black Scholar* 5 (June 1974): 2–9.

Wilkinson, Doris Y. "Toward a Positive Frame of Reference for Analysis of Black Families." *Journal of Marriage and the Family* 40 (November 1978): 707–98.

Williams, J. Allen, and Robert Stockton. "Black Family Structures and Functions: An Empirical Analysis of Some Suggestions Made by Billingsley." *Journal of Marriage and the Family* 35 (February 1973): 39–49.

About the Editor

Sr. Thea Bowman, FSPA, Ph.D., teacher by vocation and gospel singer by avocation, is consultant for intercultural awareness for the Catholic Diocese of Jackson (Mississippi). An enthusiastic presenter of nationwide workshops in cross-cultural communication, spirituality, and worship, she is also on the faculty of the Institute for Black Catholic Studies at Xavier University, New Orleans.

Sr. Thea's interest in the Black family grows out of an interest in people on the one hand and the means of human communication on the other.

"I am convinced that as we spend more time talking together, singing together, praying together, playing and working together, we grow to be family and community and Church," she says. "We have to plan ways and means to facilitate the kind of sharing that promotes that kind of growth."

Out of her interest in communication, Sr. Thea became interested in the various ways that faith and values are communicated and the relationship of culture, communication, and spirituality.

"The gift of Blackness to the Church," she reflects, "is a wholistic approach to worship and catechesis that involves memory and imagination, feeling, emotion, and passion, as well as intellect and commitment.

"I think that the spontaneity, the participation, and the joy in celebration that I learned from my people are part of my gift to the Church. Our liturgy is rich and expressive, full of movement, music, and symbols, all rooted in a deep tradition."

Jerome Friar

Design:
Diane Smirnow
Silver Spring, Md.

Original art:
Sr. Angela Williams, OSF, Ashantè Studio
Oldenburg, Ind.

Typeface:
Cheltenham light and Cheltenham bold

Typography:
EPS Group, Inc.
Baltimore, Md.

Cover photos:
Clockwise from top left: CHD/Peter Magubane; Courtesy of *Southern Cross*; Rogelio Solis/Courtesy of *Mississippi Today*; Courtesy of the John Reese Family.